Marvin, Francis
Compte, the founder
of sociology

DATE DUE

MAR 2 0			
OCT 0 7 2004			

COMTE

COMTE

THE FOUNDER OF SOCIOLOGY

By

F. S. MARVIN

"The hope in the bosom of a man whose fixed star
is Humanity, becomes a part of his blood and is
extinguished when his blood flows no more."—
GEORGE MEREDITH. *Vittoria.*

New York

RUSSELL & RUSSELL

1965

First published 1936

REISSUED, 1965, BY RUSSELL & RUSSELL, INC.

BY ARRANGEMENT WITH CHAPMAN & HALL, LTD.

L. C. CATALOG CARD NO: 65-17911

PRINTED IN THE UNITED STATES OF AMERICA

CONTENTS

Auguste Comte (Portrait) . *Frontispiece*

Contents

CHAPTER I

"CAN COMTE REALLY BE CALLED A PHILOSOPHER?"

THIS was an authentic question asked recently by a prominent Oxford teacher, when it was proposed to include Comte in a series of books on leading philosophers. The proposal was rejected. 'Tis a strange point of view, not peculiar to Oxford. It raises in the most challenging form the question of what we mean by "philosophy," or what we ought to mean. It leads straight to the subject of this book—sociology and its acknowledged founder. For if Comte is not to be considered a philosopher; sociology, which to him was the crown, both of a positive philosophy and a positive polity, remains also outside the pale. It will be necessary to deal, however briefly, with these preliminary questions before we turn to Comte himself.

It is a good thing to take first the question of what we mean by "philosophy," or "a philosopher," because throughout this book it will be found that a large part—sometimes more than half—of the difficulties and dissensions which rage about abstract questions, depend on the meaning of the terms used. "Metaphysics," "psychology," "natural laws," are examples which occur to the mind at once in connexion with Comte. The word "philosophy" has, of course, a much wider and older connotation than any of these, and there is no possible way of determining its meaning, or indeed the meaning of any term, except that of referring to those who have used it. Now in the case of philosophy, though the subject-matter contains the deepest and most acute dissensions in the world, there is no difference of opinion as to the general meaning men have attached to the word. It has always meant the seeking, and the seeing, of the general relations between things, and, on the moral side, the possession, or the cultivation, of a settled and harmonious spirit. This latter aspect of the word very happily preserves the touch of quiet and affection which the Greek implies. On the intellectual side, men of all schools of thought have always agreed that philosophy means dealing with the generalities of things. With the earliest Greek thinkers, to whom some physical objcet, such as water, or some physical quality, such as hot or cold, might seem the most general of all things, there was of course no question of dividing philosophy from science. The two were one. As time went on, and physical science increased, while at the same time men reflected more and more on the operations of their minds, there came a tendency to distinguish the two fields of thought and use philosophy only of the latter. But this restricted use of the word has never gained the consent of mankind. Men still think, and rightly think, of philosophy as the attempt to see things whole, and, as the vast mass of things presented to our minds are now the subject-matter of some branch of science, it is theoretically impossible to dissever philosophy from science. The common sense and common usage of mankind are amply justified, and it is the proper task of the academic, or trained, philosopher not to set up an enclosure for his special type of thinking, leaving the mass outside, but to study how the various special types or departments of thought are to be arranged harmoniously within the one great fold. The Oxford teacher of philosophy seemed unfortunately inclined to the former and impossible task. But the consensus of the vast majority of thinkers is against such eccentricity, whether on the general question of the nature of philosophy, or on the special question of the place of Comte in the ranks. On the latter point one testimony is so striking that it may stand alone. . . . M. Félix Ravaisson, author of a famous book on the Metaphysics of Aristotle and a profound student of philosophy of all types and ages, was chosen by M. Duruy in 1863 to write a survey of "Philosophy in France in the Nineteenth Century" for the purposes of an international exhibition then being held in Paris. This report, which might have been merely occasional and quite ephemeral, turned out to be a masterpiece and it has been studied by generations of young Frenchmen as the best account of its subject, and a good introduction to the study of philosophy as a whole. In this book Ravaisson, not himself an adherent of any school, least of all of the positivist, treats Comte's work in philosophy as the central fact of the century. He traces its antecedents and its development in Comte's own life and the way it had acted by attraction or repulsion on later thought. Comte dominates the book; and, were we to group together all that has been written about him, it would undoubtedly far exceed that on any other philosopher of his own lifetime or since. Hegel died in 1831, twenty-six years before Comte, who had sought communication with him as a young man. Since then no one, with the exception of Herbert Spencer, has attempted an encyclopedic synthesis and Spencer's has not created the same passionate or religious reactions as Comte's.

It is, therefore, a very necessary part of the history of modern thought to inquire why or how this has happened. The answer is really a short summary and anticipation of what this volume is written to explain.

It must then be assumed, from the very nature of thought as accepted and expressed in all the languages of mankind, that the essence of philosophy is seizing, or forming, connexions between facts as presented to our consciousness. This is the broadest and simplest way of stating what goes on, both in the making of science and philosophy, and philosophy must be taken to cover the widest type of generalization. In a loose and colloquial sense the word is used to denote any sort of generalizing thought or even feeling; strictly, as knowledge grows, it should be applied to the highest and most general conclusions. It is impossible, obviously, to use it of any form of thought—if such there be— which is distinct from, or independent of, what we know as "science," for the reason that all thinking is conditioned by facts studied in many branches of science. Every thought has its physical concomitant in a certain state of the brain; the brain has its biochemical constitution, and acts chemically, with the rest of the body, in accord with the physical and mechanical laws of matter or of nature. To assign, therefore, the term philosophy, as the Oxford teacher was attempting to do, to one type or section of thought relating to our mental processes but apart from science, is either a pure fiction or at the best a professional convention which has the grave disadvantage of ignoring or obscuring the essential interconnexions of things.

Now the unique position of Comte, and the explanation of the central position assigned to him by Ravaisson and a host of others who by no means accept all, or even the major part, of his conclusions, lie in this. Coming at the top of a wave of scientific discoveries, and excited also by the political and social changes in the European world around him, he conceived the idea, which was shared in varying degrees by other thinkers of his time, that science might be unified and used in such a way as to harmonize the discords of human life and give an authoritative direction to human action in future. Two sides, therefore, of his work stand out at once. They are represented in Comte's writings by his two great treatises, the *Positive*

Philosophy and the *Positive Polity* of which the former contains his synthesis based on science and the latter its application to the problems of life. The former being the more original, and arising from his own early studies both of science and history, has always been the more influential on the thought of others. It contains his first exposition of Sociology as the crown and unifying principle of all science. This is the *idée-mère* of all his thought, as it will be the main topic of this book.

We shall see later the historical genesis, the theoretical limitations and the difficulties of this principle. But it is necessary first of all to grasp what it is, its *prima-facie* appeal, how Comte saw it, and how, elaborated in detail and with intense and life-long passion, it has worked on the minds of others.

Taking the longest possible survey of the history of human thought we see various sorts of knowledge increasing constantly both in extent and in co-ordination. This, which is a commonplace of all the preachers, became a startling general reflexion after the outburst of new science in the seventeenth century. It suggested that all things were bound together in some ascertainable way which would enable men to predict their happenings, and the thought spread upwards from the inanimate to the animate sphere. In a broad and simple way it had been always known that living things followed their sequence, and could be predicted, as surely as the inanimate. Oaks had always come from acorns and animals bred according to their kind. Could the whole field of biology be brought under the same rule of natural law, and, if so, how can we exclude the human kind, which on its animal side plainly follows a similar ordering? It was here that Comte's boldness and passionate turn for synthesis came into play. At this point he saw the opportunity for the creation of a new and higher science to preside over the hierarchy of knowledge, and for the recognition of a supreme organism to embody and control it. The science is Sociology, which name he invented; and the being or organism is Humanity, acting, as he always conceived it, as an essentially united whole.

It must be said again that we are not now attempting any criticism of the idea, but merely trying to present it faithfully in its essence. Looking at it so, every one must admit the brilliance of the first illumination. That there were common features of "man," and that all men were in some sense brothers, were commonplaces of the moral philosopher from the beginning. It could not be seen, however, that this community of mankind embraced the whole order of the uniformities of nature, until that order had been established in the lower sciences, and those lower sciences shown to be the basis of human existence. The moment came in the lifetime of Auguste Comte and he was unquestionably the first person to formulate the idea.

We shall have later on to glance at the historical anticipations of the theory; still more, it will be necessary to examine somewhat closely the great underlying assumptions; first, that there is an ascertainable order in the life of humanity; and, secondly, how humanity, being itself the object of the theorizing, can at the same time conceive the theory. On the more critical side, it will be right to point out how the special mondial circumstances of Comte's career gave a bias, often an actual perversion, to his vision. And, coming to the sequel, it must be made clear that the field thus first denominated "sociology" by Comte, was so vast that no human intellect could adequately compass it; that in his own time he turned from the wider study of the area to the propagation of a highly individualist scheme for the better ordering of life in future; and that his successors, while still employing his *idée-mère* and often his own terminology, have for the most part produced a "sociology" which he would hardly recognize as his own. All that is true, and must be more or less briefly stated. But it will perhaps be generally agreed, as an introductory step: First, that the question with which we started, may be rightly answered in the affirmative. If philosophy is to retain anything of its age-long meaning, still more, if we are to look to philosophy as a reconciler of the mental dispersiveness which has gravely increased in the century since Comte, we must recognize in his synthesis an epoch-making attempt to end that dispersion. Whatever we may think of its success, it was a philosophical effort of the highest and largest kind.

Secondly—in any study of a great figure or movement or influential theory, the first, and far the most important, thing is to understand its value. Had Comte's theory no value, it would not have struck the imagination of men, or provoked so much criticism as well as following, as it did. Nothing is easier in such a case than to point to the lacunæ in the science, the errors in detail in the history, or to coin epigrams like Huxley's " Catholicism minus Christianity." It is the permanent value which we should primarily study, both in men and theories; and in the case of Comte we shall find this in his attitude towards the two master-conceptions of which the names are inseparably linked with his own—Sociology and Humanity. The first, for which he coined a hybrid word to denote our special joint debt to Greece and Rome, was to be a new and supreme creation crowning the whole structure of science. Modern thought had, since Galileo, been amassing ordered facts in unexampled array. Biology was first thought of as one great science in Comte's own lifetime. He would add, as the coping-stone, Sociology, the science of human life. But, while that word was a neologism, "Humanity" was ancient, charged with many strains and ages of emotion and morality. Comte gave it two new and profound connexions; one, with science through Sociology; the other, with religion through the practical scheme and organization which occupied all the latter part of his life. Of this we shall naturally have but little to say in this book, but it should be remembered as colouring the whole of his thought at least for the last twelve years. It is indeed remembered by all who have ever learnt anything about him. For the "Religion of Humanity" always suggests Comte's name, and the word "Humanity" has, through him, gained a fresh set of connotations either for reverence or for criticism.

In this book we have to consider it as describing the being, or the conception, which to Comte's mind made Sociology possible.

CHAPTER II

THE BACKGROUND OF COMTE'S PHILOSOPHY

IT is well understood, in any philosophical treatment of history, that all prominent men, as well as others, however much they may owe to their personal endowment, are at the same time representative of their age, inspired by their surroundings. This view is especially characteristic of the school of thought to which Comte belonged. The doctrine of the *milieu* expresses it, and has sometimes led its followers, especially Taine, to extravagant lengths, as in his *History of English Literature*. Comte must, of course, be looked at through his own glasses and would have asked for nothing else. What then was the dominant factor in the European environment in which his mind was formed?

Comte and his contemporaries, especially in France, were under the shadow of the Revolution. He was born in 1798, and we shall see in the next chapter the family influences which played on his youth. The social, religious and political circumstances of the time were all profoundly disturbed, as they have never been in England. It seemed that all old institutions had been overthrown and that a new world was to be built on the ruins. In particular the religious organization, and the religion which was identified with it, had suffered from the assaults of the revolutionists. Voltaire's injunction of *Ecrasez l'infâme* appeared to have been obeyed to the letter. Inevitably, keen and socially minded men looked elsewhere for principles on which to found a new system both of thought and of living, and to save society. In this Comte and his predecessor, St. Simon, were at one; and many more. Among the Catholics, thinkers arose, like Joseph de Maistre, who strove to breathe a new life and meaning into the old forms, and with these Comte on his practical side had much in common.

We shall see in a moment the more permanent factors which went to the making of his philosophy, but it is necessary to dwell for a little on the influence of the Revolution, because it has not been duly appraised by those who have written or thought about him. We may find a useful analogy in our own times. The Great War was a convulsion in some ways greater than the French Revolution. All writers and thinkers since the War show some marks of its influence; many of them are entirely inspired by it. It has made men think that

22

institutions and leading thoughts of pre-War days, if not obsolete, are at least all open to question. Progress, capitalism, representative government, are all treated, somewhat as the hot-heads of the Revolution treated the Ancien Régime, though sober men are well aware that the great achievements of the nineteenth century will go on and bear their fruit, much as the historian finds that the backbone of French life and government remained the same after the Revolution as before. The excitements of such a crisis stimulate active minds to great thoughts, as the War stimulated Mr. Wells to his *Outline of History*. But the permanent forces go on steadily doing their work, in spite of Robespierre, Napoleon or the Kaiser.

Just as we may read the effects of the War in any writer of our time who deals with human affairs, so in Comte the French Revolution, besides being a stimulus to thought and activity, left deep traces in the form which that thought and activity assumed. It made him give much sharper outlines and distinctions to things than their natural evolution would warrant. Though the future was to be a paradise of peace, the present and the recent past tended to be peopled with somewhat spectral forms engaged in a necessary and internecine strife. It was largely an echo of the conflicts of the

23

Revolution. In this way "*l'esprit théologique*" or "*la métaphysique*" or "psychology" assume a sharpness of outline and a self-activity which does not properly belong to them, and which is still less true of them in later times than in Comte's. The crowning example of this attitude is to be found in his forecast of the future of his own system of reorganization. Within fifty years this should have overcome all obstacles and be established as the new religion and republic of the West. But the normal development of things is far otherwise, and these normal features have become much clearer to us than they were to him. The longer society lasts, and the more it is sustained and organized by science, the less catastrophic will be the changes. The Christian churches absorb new ideas and transform themselves instead of giving place to a rival institution based entirely on the new. The State everywhere performs many functions which in Comte's ideal should have been left to the Spiritual Power, or individual and disinterested men. And so throughout his clear-cut system. Nothing, either on the scientific or the practical side, is found to be so well defined or independent as his analysis would suggest—Astronomy in relation to physics and chemistry; logic to mathematics; psychology linking biology and sociology; the species, both of plants and animals, actually passing into one another in the process of time.

All tell the same tale, but it will be understood that this is a criticism not of the substantial truths contained in his ideas, but of the form of their presentation. In this sense specially he was the child of his age, and in view of the analogies between the crisis in his days and our own, the fact should rather commend him to our study.

But in a much deeper sense Comte thought and wrote as the spokesman of his times.

The end of the eighteenth century was a notable point in the building up of science, and how little that process can be identified with the revolutionary storms which swept the surface, may be gathered from the fate of Condorcet and Lavoisier, two of the master-builders. What had been growing in the consciousness of men since men began to think, came at that time to a culmination and decisive expression. Of this we may be as well assured as we are that Comte invented the word "sociology," and founded that branch of science. Of the nature of that growth and how far Comte's work may rightly be considered as following from it, we shall have to speak more fully in a later chapter. Here we can only shortly indicate the background. The ancient world had achieved a marvellous apparatus

25

of mathematical reasoning, mainly relating to geometrical forms. It had mapped out the heavens in the light of its geometry, and had gained some insight into the nature of human health (with Hippocrates) and into the nature of animal life (with Aristotle). Then came a long pause, between the extinction of ancient science and its revival in the fifteenth century. That thousand years were by no means unfruitful, and Comte was one of the first and strongest to lay stress on their accomplishments. But for the building of science they made little direct contribution, and, when Copernicus in the fifteenth and Galileo in the sixteenth century took up the thread, the main structure had still to be worked out. By the seventeenth century, acute and scientific thinkers, such as Francis Bacon and Descartes, began to gain some general idea of what was going on. By that time physical science could be contemplated as a whole and contrasted with the dogmas and perverted Aristotelianism which had come down from the Middle Ages. The vision opened up a vista of science applied and human life ameliorated. Still the structure was in its infancy. Most of the branches of science as we know it to-day, had not yet been thought of, and those in existence were only sketched out. Mathematics had received the inestimable benefit of the calculus.

Geometry had become analytic. Astronomy had been extended and unified by the telescope and by Newton. Mechanics and physics had been put on a rational basis by Galileo. Men were experimenting in chemistry. Biology, except for Harvey's fundamental discovery, was still to make; both the name and the general conceptions of the science had not yet appeared. But by the end of the eighteenth century, when Comte began to think about the problem, the scene was largely changed.

To his opening mind science, that is, ordered and verified knowledge, appeared as already forming itself into several great divisions, interconnected and yet distinct. To those we have mentioned, were now added chemistry, made scientific by Lavoisier who had died by the guillotine four years before Comte's birth, and biology now taking shape through the labours of Linnæus who had died twenty years before, and Lamarck who was publishing his great works during Comte's boyhood. To Lamarck was due the name "biology," invented some ten or twelve years before Comte's "sociology." Already therefore the ordering spirit of science had passed from the inanimate to the animate sphere. Now man is clearly an animal. Is an ordered knowledge of his nature to be treated as an item in a general biology? If so, how far can

27

we claim, or expect, to have an ordered knowledge of all that Man stands for? Or is there to be another science special to man's nature and history, and, if so, how far can that go, and what is its relation to the general science of life, under which, to some extent at least, Man, being an animal, must be considered? Here we have a few of the gravest questions which this book will have to touch on in later pages. At present, dealing with the background of Comte's thought, we have only to note how the facts first presented themselves to him, and, in a summary way, the decision which he took. He decided, as soon as he grasped the facts, that there must be also a science of men as such, but in this case the man is to be treated, not as an individual, at least in the first instance, but as a "man in society." This science must always be social, called, as he first thought of it, social physics, later sociology. The idea was conceived before 1822, probably in his twentieth or one-and-twentieth year. It became from that moment the governing idea of his life, and none of those critics who have severed themselves most decidedly from his work, as the high priest of Humanity, have ever suggested any wavering in his fidelity to a belief in sociology as the science of a progressive humanity. How this progress was to be ascertained and formulated; how

in future we should equip ourselves the better to
promote it: these are questions on which men may
be sharply divided. We shall have occasion to
speak of them in later chapters.

But it will be asked at once how far Comte in
this matter was a pioneer. He was undoubtedly the
first to conceive an ordered science of man's affairs
and history, as a part and crown of general science.
He was also the first to name it. But men must
have been thinking of such questions and formulating some conclusions before him. These should
form the most immediate and active part of his
intellectual environment, and he was in fact never
backward in acknowledging such influence. To
sketch it fully would be to give an outline of the
philosophical aspect of historical thought and
writing from Herodotus to the French Revolution.
We must be content to indicate where men had
reached on the two capital points which lie at the
root of Comte's sociology. One is, the possibility
of ascertaining any connexions or sequences in
human events comparable to those which had been
ascertained in physical science. Comte's first title
for sociology, viz., "social physics," shows that in
his view the possibility was complete. There was
natural law supreme in both, nay, all domains.
The other main point, connected though indepen-

dent, is the goal which this law, if it can be ascertained, seems to indicate for human existence. Most thinkers before Comte, certainly those with whom he was best acquainted, were coming to connect the two beliefs in one dogma of inevitable progress. But there is obviously no such necessary connexion between the two beliefs. One may quite well believe that all human happenings are inevitably determined, without holding that this determination tends to a necessary increase, either in happiness or in virtue. Comte himself frequently refers to the two thinkers who had contributed most to form his mind on both aspects of this supreme question; Montesquieu and Condorcet.

The story of course goes further back than that. When, in the seventeenth century, men came, under the guidance of the new science, to appreciate the general orderliness of the physical world, the bolder minds went on at once to postulate a universal prevalence of law in the whole cosmos, including man. Such thoughts are to be found in Descartes, Hobbes and especially Spinoza. The real task, however, was not to formulate the principle, but to work it out in the actual events of man's evolution on earth and its connexions with other facts, both physical and animate. Here is the whole scope of sociology, a *scientia scientiarum*.

Those who first approached the subject, thought mainly of the influence of climate and physical conditions on human life. Montesquieu and Condorcet, being famous and recent Frenchmen, naturally came most into Comte's field of vision, and each was interesting as laying emphasis on a different aspect of the problem. Montesquieu, though primarily a lawyer and constitutional historian, laid special stress on the climatic conditions which affect society. He is emphatic on the similarity of the relations which obtain between material objects and those observable in human affairs. "Laws," he says in his greatest work on "The Spirit of Laws," "are the necessary relations following from the nature of things. . . . Between two bodies in movement the relations of mass and velocity determine the increase or diminution of movement; through every variation there is uniformity and constancy. Similar relations are to be found in human affairs." But he had no conception of a general law of change, leading to continued improvement. The view was what Comte called later "static," and for the "dynamic" idea he was most indebted to Condorcet. He might have found it, as he afterwards discovered, in Kant, and no doubt fragmentarily in other places. But Condorcet gave it in that glowing form which was characteristic of the best minds in the Revolution, and sanctified it by a martyr's death. That Condorcet's view too was imperfect and in some points perverted, was of course inevitable. How could it be possible for a mind, first possessed of a great vision piercing into the future, to present at the same time a complete and well-balanced view of all the past?

The fact that it was an ardent and disinterested revolutionist who kindled the strongest beacon which lightened Comte's path, confirms what was said at the beginning of this chapter. We may now sum up briefly the general position, from which his philosophy arose, putting the wider aspects, and letting the particular circumstances lead up to his life itself.

Science had been growing mightily since the recovery of Greek letters, and the discovery of a range of thought outside that covered by the ecclesiastical discipline of a thousand years. The fact that the new knowledge had been fiercely opposed at several stages by the organized forces of the Church—e.g., in the cases of Giordano Bruno and Galileo—made most men think that such an internecine conflict was a necessary state of things. By the end of the eighteenth century, the corpus of new knowledge had been enlarged by the constitution of a scientific chemistry and the outline of an orderly biology. While this was in process, a long violent outbreak took place in France, which though it had many substantial and material causes, raged most bitterly over the rights of the Church and the social order bound up with it. To a thinker bent on peace and brooding always most intently over the difference of beliefs rather than of interests, it was of the first moment to present a coherent doctrine which might reconcile all. This must, as it seemed, arise from science, which had been growing steadily, while the authority of the Church had diminished and had just been successfully challenged in arms. Complete therefor the structure of science, so that its teaching may cover all the ground which the Church had claimed. The man who put his hand to this task was born of a devout Catholic and Royalist family in 1798, while the beaten Church was still under the Civil Constitution of the clergy.

CHAPTER III

WE saw in the last chapter that Comte was born just after the most violent phase of the French Revolution, and he grew up while Napoleon was attempting what Comte always regarded as a reactionary and nefarious use of dictatorial power. His father was cashier at the tax office in the Department of Hérault and lived at Montpellier. His mother was a Boyer, and both parents were of a strongly conservative turn, which meant, at that time and place, Catholic and Royalist. The boy was sent at the age of nine to the "college" at Montpellier, where at once he revealed the determined character which distinguished him through life. He learnt quickly and voraciously. He submitted to, and adored, those of his masters who seemed to him to possess any moral or intellectual superiority. He revolted constantly against authority imposed as such. Being precocious in mathematics, he passed the examination for the École Polytechnique in Paris a year before the accustomed time, and employed the interval at his old school in giving advanced and perfectly coherent lectures to the other scholars in the mathematical division. In 1814 he went to Paris, and soon established his primacy among the students of his time. In 1816 he became the ringleader in a protest against one of the staff whose manners had offended the independent spirit of the class. The École was for a time sent down, but Comte's residence and profession for life were settled by the event. He resolved, much against his parents' wish, to be a private teacher of mathematics and live in Paris. He obtained later on a post at the École itself, when re-established, and was for several years both one of the staff and an examiner for entrance at various provincial centres. There were also occasional attempts at other occupations—e.g., a few months as private secretary to Casimir Périer. But the teaching of mathematics to private pupils was always his standby, and there are amusing accounts extant of the precision and thoroughness with which he carried out that work. If only it had been certain and sufficiently well paid, it would have suited him well, for it imposed no external authority and left him free to follow his own bent in study and writing.

Three events in the earlier portion of his life in Paris—each highly characteristic of the man—call for special notice. Each had a profound bearing on the development of his thought.

The first was his association of six years—from 1818 to 1824—with St.-Simon. This had a strong influence, much debated ever since, on the initial direction of his philosophy. In estimating Comte's life and work it is necessary to form some opinion as to this influence.

The second was his marriage with Caroline Massin which took place in 1825, after his breach with St.-Simon. It was important in its sequel and also, in all its incidents, displayed Comte as a man of scrupulous conduct according to his own ideas of moral and legal obligation. The failure of the marriage prepared him for the passionate adoration of another woman which filled the latter portion of his life.

The third was his final breach with the École Polytechnique and the official world generally, which threw him in his later years on to the generosity of private persons for his support, and did much to constitute him in his own circle as the high priest of a new religion. It also brought out and accentuated in his mind the supremacy which he claimed over mathematics for the new

science which he was to found. The official professors were for the supremacy, or at least the
independence, of mathematics. For Comte sociology was to take control.

Each of these episodes must be briefly considered.
The Comte Henri de St.-Simon was a man
nearly forty years older than Auguste Comte. He
was, of course, of noble birth, ambitious, ingenious
and philanthropic. He had already distinguished
himself by various deeds and schemes before the
end of the eighteenth century. He had served in
the American War of Independence; he had pro-
jected a Panama canal; above all, he had conceived
a plan for the reorganization of society on the
basis of science and industry. He was one of those
noted in the last chapter on whom the nightmare of
the Revolution pressed most hard. He even
appealed to the restored Louis XVIII to restore the
whole State on his new and improved pattern.
Industrial chiefs were to take the place of military
feudalists, and the doctrines of science to replace
the dogmas of the Church. The analogy with
certain broad features of Comte's later teaching is
obvious, and it is obvious also that the early meeting of such a famous and interesting senior must
have been a powerful stimulus to the young and
eager aspirant, just settled in Paris in 1818. Comte

himself in the earlier period of his relationship described St.-Simon's action as having "launched" him. Their mutual interactions later on have been a profitless subject for minute study by many writers; for the general equation is clear enough. Comte being a much better trained, more acute and consistent mind, welcomed the early sympathy, absorbed whatever suited him into his own system, and then rejected a patronage which tended to present to the public all Comte's writings as being merely the transcriptions of St.-Simon's thought. The issue was inevitable, given the character of the two men. The sequel, down to our own time, is an instructive commentary on the original relation. Comte developed as a systematic thinker, and, as we saw in the first chapter, has been treated ever since as a landmark in the history of nineteenth-century philosophy. The one part of his later work in which, though with different formulæ, he returned to St.-Simonian ideas—namely the organization of a new religious body—has proved the least successful.

The episode of his marriage, which followed the breach with St.-Simon in 1824, need not detain us long, for by that time the main lines of his philosophy had been well laid down, and his wife cannot be said to have had any direct influence on his

thought. She deserves, however, some thanks
from those who prize his work, for her sensible
and effective action at the time of his mental break-
down in 1826. His digestive organs were always
feeble, and he was at that time exceptionally
excited by a dispute which had arisen with one of
St.-Simon's followers as to the ownership of certain
ideas which had been published in the St.-Simonian
organ. Comte's reason for a time gave way, and
he was confined in a large asylum from which his
wife rescued him for private treatment at home. He
recovered completely after one or two really
dangerous events, and though he separated from
his wife in 1842, he continued a friendly correspondence, was always grateful for her early action,
and in his most straitened circumstances made an
allowance for her maintenance. One should not
in these circumstances lay too much stress on the
previous moral lapses or immoral status of either
party, and the fact that the whole of the first great
work, the *Positive Philosophy*, was written while
they were living together, shows that the relations
were not at all times intolerable. But two other
points are equally clear about this relationship.
The first, that it was far from being an intellectual
or emotional partnership. At best it was merely
friendly and worldly. The other, that, feeling the

deficiency, and becoming, as we shall see, more and more introspective in later years, Comte was prepared for the complete emotional surrender of himself to Clothilde de Vaux from 1845 to the end.

The episode of the loss of his appointments at the École Polytechnique, and his recurrence to private subscription for his support, has a theoretical interest, in so far as it arose out of jealousy on the part of mathematicians, and a strong practical interest, in so far as it led to the institution of the "*subside sacerdotal*" and, through the continuance of this after his death, to the maintenance of a form of religious organization.

The story begins with the publication of the amazing preface to the last volume of the *Positive Philosophy* in 1842. This contains already all the features of intense self-confidence and hostility to those who were not prepared to accept either himself or his views as he had been expounding them for twenty years which gradually developed in him. It complains bitterly of the neglect which had compelled him to great privations and hard private work, at the same time as he was elaborating his philosophy. It demands as of right that the public, especially the French public, should put his due support out of doubt, and that, in particular, the annual elections required for his posts at the Ecole should in future be waived. It is not surprising that the demand had exactly the opposite effect from that intended. The geometers at the school, who formed the most active part of the electorate and who are especially attacked in the preface, gathered to themselves the majority of the other—official and specialist—voters, and he was not only refused the position of security which he asked but was gradually deprived of all the posts which he had held. The publisher of the book most improperly introduced, without Comte's authority or knowledge, a note disclaiming this preface. A lawsuit followed in which, on this definite legal point as between author and publisher, Comte naturally gained the day with damages. But it was a Pyrrhic triumph, for the substantial points for which the preface was written, were lost beyond recall. There was of course the wider appeal to men of means and good-will who sympathized with the plight of the philosopher, however much they may have deplored the unwisdom of his action. Such were found at first in England, where, through Mill's vigorous support, subscriptions were raised from three or four wealthy men which for a time made up for the loss of Comte's official income. When this was dropped—much to Comte's indignation—

Littré came forward in Paris and headed a more general subscription list which was maintained from various smaller sources until his death and after. The last period of his life covers ten years till his death in 1857. It covers, therefore, the revolution of 1848, at which time Comte issued a manifesto constituting an "Association libre pour l'instruction positive du peuple dans tout l'Occident européen," with the motto "Order and Progress." It covers also the great emotional event of his life, in his personal intercourse with Clothilde de Vaux for just over a year, and his worship of her memory ever after. The year was 1845, and to that crowning episode we must now turn for a few moments.

He had separated, as we saw, from his wife in 1842. At the end of 1844 he met at the house of one of his pupils and admirers, a young married lady, the sister of the pupil. Her maiden name was Marie and she was married to a man called de Vaux who was serving a life sentence for defalcation of tax money which it was his office to collect. She was a beautiful, intelligent and sympathetic person and had, after the forced separation from her criminal husband, formed another attachment from which, on moral grounds, she had just torn herself, when she met Comte. They were certainly well adapted to one another, for she was clearly a

42

gentle and reasonable nature, deep enough to appreciate his thought, artistic enough to supplement him on the side where his training had been most scant. As passionate friends they passed the remaining sixteen months of her life in constant correspondence and frequent visits. To Comte, who in pursuance of his *hygiène cérébrale* maintained to the end his reading of a few classics, she became as the Beatrice of Dante. After her death there was no other comparable friend. He lived more and more on the memory of his love and in his hopes of human reconstruction.

It is interesting to note that the life which we are describing falls in its maturity into three roughly comparable parts. There are the first six years of seminal work, of formative and seething ideas, with St.-Simon as the leading outside figure. After the violent breach with St.-Simon, comes the long middle period of hardest continued intellectual output, in which his wife is undoubtedly the main outside figure, saving him in the time of his madness and, though often irritating and increasingly unsympathetic, yet keeping a constant domestic centre for his work. Then the last stage of rapture and absorption in the ideal, which at this point can happily be combined with the one outside figure who commanded his thoughts and devotion.

43

It does not fall within the scope of a book describing Comte as the founder of sociology, to speak at any length of the latest period of his life. The work of foundation had been done long before. He did not add to his scientific material in the later years, nor did he ever consciously alter the scientific and philosophic conclusions reached in the earlier works. What happened was, that his new emotional disposition suffused a new tone to all he wrote and thought. What he loved and approved of, was seen in a halo. All who had opposed or criticized him, were regarded as definitely hostile. His position, as the head of a new religious organization, was sanctified and strengthened in his own mind. M. Ravaisson, in the book referred to in the opening chapter, seizes gladly on Comte's exaltation of the emotions in his later work, and from M. Ravaisson's own point of view it is natural enough. For the goal of Ravaisson's philosophy was an Infinite Love, realizing itself in the Universe and, most conspicuously to us, in the heroic man. To this Comte's period of passionate love and disciplined life seemed to bring him nearer. So far as this follows from the application of his sociology, something may be said about it later on. But it was not one of the formative influences which created sociology in the mind of the young thinker. He was full then of the ideas which had made science triumphant in so many spheres and his mastering passion was to bring the facts of human society into a similar order, so that the new and supreme science might crown the whole. How this was done, and how far it is a valid enterprise, is the main topic of this book.

From the first, owing to the intense self-concentration of the thinker, he had a tendency to treat his conclusions not as a contribution to thought, but as a settled doctrine to be propagated and not altered. The *hygiène cérébrale* of which we spoke above, was in operation long before the time in which he applied it to Clothilde de Vaux. It consisted in abstention from the reading of current literature, especially of periodicals, and the exclusive study of a few masterpieces of the past. The effect on the "doctrine" was obvious, and the emotional absorption in Clothilde heightened the colours of the apotheosis. In the last stage we are brought face to face in sharpest outlines with the contradiction between a church, or permanent organization of any kind, based on a set of definite beliefs or dogmas, and the incessant change of belief and growth of knowledge outside. One must recognize a clear element of value on each

side of the antithesis, just as the soul of an individual or of a nation must keep its identity and
stability, while all the elements, both of its environment and its nature, change with time. In the case
of Comte's sociology, no school of later sociologists
would accept it as it stands. Yet, as we shall see,
a great kernel of permanent truth remains, besides
many brilliant *aperçus* thrown off in the labour of
working out the whole by that amazing process of
mental concentration which he practised. The
result has something of the effect of a great work
of art, grim and rugged in this case, but with clear-
cut and impressive features. In the history of art
such works often produce an adoration which is
inclined to treat them as the final expression of the
thing they profess to portray. Then comes a
reaction and rebellious spirits who refuse to bow
down to anything as perfect, proceed to dissect
and vilify the whole. Even the Greeks and
Raphael have been treated in that temper. Comte's
sociology, though certainly less perfect than a
Greek statue, has also lines true to life and worthy
of careful study. Its strength as well as its limitations were due, in the first place, to the strongly
marked character of the thinker, then to the historical conditions of his time, and, lastly, to those
personal accidents which have just been sketched.

CHAPTER IV

THE ROOT IDEA OF COMTE'S SOCIOLOGY

IT is not an uncommon thing to meet "educated" people who question the fact of there being any "laws" of social phenomena. Even a stray sociologist has been known to commit himself to this form of incredulity. As the existence of such "laws" is the cardinal, or starting, point in Comte's sociology, we may be thankful to the sceptics for raising it. It is a large and most complicated question, still further obscured by the ambiguity of language. The same word has come to be used for the commands of a law-giver that such and such things should be done at the risk of a prescribed penalty, and for those observed uniformities of happening, whether in the physical or animal world, which men have been formulating ever since science began. In the latter sense of "law," men have been for centuries extending the reign of ordered sequence in what they observe. They passed from simple examples, such as the fall

47

of the stone or the movements of the planets, to the more involved, such as the expansion of gases, the combination of molecules to make various substances and the growth of plants and animals from germs. In all these cases they had been able to formulate in terms of more or less precision, the relation of the facts observed, the "law" of their sequence, so as to be able to predict, from a given state of things at a certain time, what would appear thereafter. Comte claimed to have added human events to the rest. When it was seen that everything which happened, human and other, was equally describable in terms which may be called "laws" and was so far capable of being predicted, Man would have entered into his kingdom. The mind which had discovered these laws, would, by obeying and using them, be able to foresee and, within certain limits, command the future. It was the last extension of Bacon's famous maxim and by its truth Comte would certainly have been glad to stand or fall. As being of this decisive character, the principle calls for some searching examination on the threshold of any judgment of Comte's work. It becomes still more urgent when we are told by a modern sociologist that the idea has been abandoned, and when, as now, one hears in almost every scientific discussion of a general kind that the position of the principle of determination is now quite indeterminate.

The debate on all these points is of course profound. It is indeed the largest which can be raised on any philosophic question, and in a few pages one can but briefly indicate conclusions which rest on ages of controversy and treatises without number. It may perhaps simplify what one has to say here about it, as a preliminary to Comte's sociology, if one divides the topic into three parts, or distinguishes three aspects of it. In the first place, there is the quite recent discovery of what appears to certain physicists, Sir Arthur Eddington for instance, as the overthrow of the principle of determinable law in the realm of physics itself, where it was supposed to be firmly established and whence it had spread to other spheres. In the second place, comes the question as to how far and by what means we can reasonably extend the principle, however amended, to the facts of life and, above all, of human society. Lastly, one must end on a note of awe—agnosticism, if you will—at the supreme mystery that it is the human mind itself, which is supposed to be subject to this determination, which has discovered and lays down the law.

On the first, and most recent aspect, of the

controversy the physicists themselves, having discovered the dilemma, have of late become fairly
unanimous in indicating the way by which we may
extricate ourselves from it. It is now a matter of
common knowledge that the smallest material
entities to which physical analysis has reduced the
universe, do not appear to follow any determinable
path. If you fix their location, you cannot fix their
velocity, and vice versa. The universe of infini-
tesimals, thus revealed to us, becomes in fact a
ceaseless and apparently aimless maze. Where the
older scientific vision had seen an orderly march
as of the sun and heavenly bodies above us, the new
revelation is of a meaningless tangle within, around
and, above all, beneath us, for it would deprive us
of the solid earth on which we stand. The answer
now given by the indeterminate physicists themselves is that, though one cannot depend theoretically on any regularity of behaviour in the material
world, *statistically* we may. Thus, in a famous
example, though we have every right to expect
that the particles of water in a kettle on the fire
might group themselves into a solid mass of ice, and
that undoubtedly they would do so, if we continued the experiment to infinity, statistically, and
for practical purposes, we may be content to
predict evaporation at 100° C. The solution of the

difficulty is sufficient not only for practical life but for the present argument. Although, as Sir Arthur Eddington has told us, "The path of the Earth through space is as she pleases," no one on this account has cast any doubts on the Nautical Almanac or ceased to cultivate according to the seasons.

When we pass from the phenomena of the physical world to those of life, and especially of human society, an interesting reflexion must occur to us, arising from this recent re-formulation of our conceptions of the physical. We should look, we are now told, rather to statistics than to any inherent necessity, to explain the observed regularities of nature. But that is precisely the ground which has already been taken up by many of the deepest thinkers on human problems. The oft-quoted statement of Immanuel Kant[1] embodies that idea. It will be remembered that he says, "However one may wish metaphysically to assert or represent the freedom of the will, its manifestations in human actions are determined like any other natural phenomenon by the general laws of nature. History, which occupies itself with the recital of these manifestations, never renounces the

[1] "The Idea of a Universal History from the point of view of Humanity" (1784).

51

hope of discovering their causes however profoundly concealed they may be. The fact is that when we consider the operation of freewill on the large scale, we discover in them a regular movement, and what appears in the individual to be confused and irregular, is seen, in the species, as a continual but slow development of the original dispositions of mankind. Thus marriages, births and deaths, when regarded in the individual case, appear subject to no law which would enable us beforehand to calculate their number. Yet the annual tables which are drawn up in all great countries, prove that there are in this sphere also laws of occurrence as constant as those observed in atmospheric variations. The latter also cannot be foreseen at any given point, but in the mass they operate regularly and without interruption and produce the growth of plants, the course of rivers and all the rest of the natural economy."

Here again is the statistical point of view, announced with regard to human events a hundred and fifty years ago. The analogy is striking, but must not be allowed to hurry us into any identification of the human with the physical which would justly be regarded as materialistic. All we may conclude is that there is a superficial resemblance in the methods of arriving at general results in both cases. Uniformities in the mass cannot be denied or disregarded, and have some explanation which we cannot yet formulate in a completely rational or mechanical way. The human case has, however, many other aspects.

In a first, and quite obvious everyday sense, we do predict and therefore do believe and assert a certain, or at least an accepted, sequence of events in human as in physical events. Men make their wills with as much confidence that they will sometime die, as they expect the rising and setting of the sun. All human intercourse is based on such a belief. Tradesmen supply us with goods expecting payment, judges confine criminals in gaol to punish previous and prevent future offences, in the same spirit. History and sociology, however, are concerned with the actions of numerous men acting together, and here, according to Kant's statistical observations, the adherence to rule should be closer and prediction more within our powers. In one sense, as Kant points out, this is so; in another, however, it is more difficult to predict. Thus, while we are certain of the death of individual men, we are by no means certain as to the future conduct and fate of collections of men, e.g., of a nation. Who, for instance, could have predicted the revival of the Polish nation as the result of a World War in 1914 or indeed have been confident that Poland would ever arise again from her abasement and the mutilation of the eighteenth century? There seems to be some sort of contradiction here, and Kant's dictum requires some further examination. He is speaking of the levelling out of large numbers of things that happen at different times and ways to individuals. This is the essence of the statistical or actuarial method. He does not, at least in the passage quoted, refer to things happening to a large number as a whole, which are the main subject of history or sociology. The birth, the fortunes, the decay or dissolution of a nation belong to this latter class. Are we then to say that a different type of reasoning belongs to these, and that the actions of men which, as we have seen, are within certain limits predictable in their individual capacity, when they come together into a society, generate something which transcends all prediction, i.e., that there is no law in social events?

The way out of the dilemma will be found to be much on the lines which Comte himself indicates, however much we may be inclined to differ sometimes from the form of locution which he employs, oftener perhaps from the application he may make of a general theory to a particular event in history. We are not now discussing, it will be observed, the supposed freedom of the will; that is, in its ordinary acceptance on individual question; and as to individuals one must be prepared with Kant to recognize regularities on a large scale. The question now is what is the difference, from the standpoint of regularity and prediction, between individual and collective happenings. There would seem to be two main kinds of difference, each no doubt making the social problem more difficult than the individual, but neither fundamentally altering its character. The first is, the far greater complexity which at once arises as we multiply the objects of our study. The other, that man in society actually generates something independent of his individual will, which acts upon him above his own volitions, and may be, or may not be, susceptible of study and prediction as the individual is. He is in it and helps to make it, but it is more than either he, or any other of his fellows. How is this to be studied, and can we find any regularities about it and predict its movements? This is the question which must chiefly engage our attention when rendering an account of Comte's thought, because it is precisely this super-individual thing, especially in the form which he exalted as Humanity, of which he is constantly thinking and speaking.

The case of Poland is an excellent example for both types of difference between the individual and the social. Its complexity is obvious. The fate of the country, or of its people, depended not only on the geographical conditions and the personal endowment and actions of its individual inhabitants, but upon those of its neighbours and the innumerable possible contacts between them. Actually no one could have predicted with any certainty the partition of Poland in the manner and at the time when it happened. Still less could one have foreseen the resurrection in 1919 which depended on a still wider field of incident and influence. The actual event was striking evidence of the reality and force of the other, super-individual, factors which come into play in sociology and social history. No doubt the resurrection was conditioned by a conjuncture of external causes and by the arising of an individual, Pilsudski, strong enough to make use of them. Without these it would be impossible to assume the functioning of the super-individual factor. But without the idea of the nation enshrined in, yet acting upon the individual above and beyond himself, the external factors would not have produced the result they did. The nation-idea can itself be historically traced. When established, it proceeds to operate as a fresh force determining individual action. In all Comte's sociology this type of force plays a leading rôle, and no doubt the intensity of his faith often tends to a biased view both of the past and still more of the future. Yet if there is to be a sociology at all, it must look mainly to the growth of social factors. Hence the sociological prediction in the case of Poland would have been that, given the favourable conjuncture of circumstances, which was not impossible, the nation, based on common blood, language, habitat and history, would again assert itself. A prediction, it may be said, hedged by so many conditions can be of little use for conduct. That is a contention to which we shall return.

But before any detailed criticism is attempted it is well to make clear to ourselves and others what Comte's own position was as to both aspects of "law" in relation to human development in society, i.e., on the one side, the exceeding and growing complexity of the particular facts, and, on the other, the growth and action of something socially collective, controlling the individual. He leaves us in no doubt under either heading, and especially on the second point emphasizes and reiterates unceasingly. It is the *idée-mère* of his whole life and system. On the first point he is less detailed or insistent. But the following passage written in 1824 leaves no doubt of his position. "Pour moi, je ne me trouve jusqu'à present, après cette lecture (i.e., of Kant's essay quoted above) d'autre valeur que celle d'avoir systematisé et arrêté la conception ébauchée par Kant à mon insu." He therefore accepts with regard to the particular qualities and actions of human beings what we have described above as the statistical method. Without going into the metaphysics of freewill, which he would have regarded as an inaccessible, if not an inconceivable, question, he notes, that, studied after the event in the gross, they show such uniformities of occurrence as justify us in treating them as subject to law in the same sense, though with a less degree of possible accuracy, as the facts of the physical world. They represent the last stage in the scale of simple to complex, which, as we shall see later, seemed to him to be the right governing idea for the classification of the sciences. Meanwhile, on the side of the social force which deals with this growing complexity of circumstance, there is to be discerned in history a parallel—Comte would certainly have said a greater—growth in the human element which copes with it. Both are subject to a law of growth, of which we cannot discern the source, although we are certain on historical evidence of the reality of the process. There is thus a permanently unresolved dualism in the process of things; on the one side, the complex of events, on the other, the growing collective force of humanity, correlating them in thought, and mastering them in action. He did not look for any single principle or entity to bring the whole into an absolute unity. The unification was a progressive thing, and always imperfect; but it had its source in the steady development of collective thinking, feeling and acting among men, and the law of this growth is the supreme thing in the known universe and acknowledged by Comte as the master idea in his philosophy. On this he says:[1] "Le type fondamental de l'évolution humaine, aussi bien individuelle que collective, est scientiquement représenté comme consistent toujours dans l'ascendant croissant de notre humanité sur notre animalité, d'après la double suprématie de l'intelligence sur les penchants, et de l'instinct sympathique sur instinct personel."

This, therefore, is the cardinal principle of Comte's sociology, and both those who attack and those

[1] *Philosophic Positive*, p. 837.

59

who defend him, must in truth and justice address
themselves first to this. It will be our business later
to examine some of its consequences and applications in Comte's own works. It will be seen, for
instance, to comprise the much more often discussed "law of the three stages"; and it will be
seen also to colour very strongly his reading of
particular periods and personages in history. But
it is essential first of all to examine the general
idea in itself, and to decide whether or not it has
any *prima facie* appearance of being well founded.
Above all, it is necessary to understand what it
means. It may well be that like many other great
generalizations it is a stroke of intuitive genius and
substantially true, though capable of, and needing
constant restatement and modification in detail
and in application. Such has been the fate of
Newton's greatest law and Darwin's conception
of biological evolution.

Two or three main features stand out in the
statement of the law which is given above and
which might be paralleled from a hundred other
passages in Comte's writings. The first, and perhaps most important, is that the law is dynamic
rather than static. It describes a steady change or
growth, something constantly going on rather
than the necessary conditions and relations of

existing things. This feature of his fundamental idea was often pointed out by Comte himself; the dynamical aspect gradually absorbing and controlling the static in the study of human affairs as it had done in mechanics. It will be noticed that this feature puts him in accord with the historical spirit of the age which was taking shape clearly during his own lifetime and to which doubtless his own spirit largely contributed. It is still more strongly emphasized in the evolutionary doctrine in biology to which Darwin gave currency and triumph in the decade which followed Comte's death. Comte himself, while appreciating the work of Lamarck, the greatest pioneer of evolution in the biological world, had not felt himself able, on the evidence then available, to accept the notion of the gradual change and evolution of species. Had he been able to accept it, it would have added still more force to his general argument. On the other hand, while bringing him close to later ideas both in history and biology, Comte's master-thought is certainly not in accord with the mass of later work in sociology itself. While it is not true, as stated by the speaker quoted at the opening of this chapter, that later sociologists deny all laws in human affairs, for this would at once destroy their science, it is true that they have as a rule departed

from Comte's main interest which was the discovery of evolutionary laws in history, and have
turned mainly to the study and accumulation of
social facts. In this respect Herbert Spencer has
been a more powerful influence since his death
than Comte. American work in sociology is
largely of this character and the mass of material
put together by anthropologists like Sir James
Frazer. It would no doubt be held by most of
them that the spade-work of collection had still far
to go before we can draw any conclusions as to an
evolutionary law. The want of such law is also
apparent in the bulk of historical collections of a
general kind of which Oswald Spengler is a
conspicuous example.

The second main feature noticeable in Comte's
law goes far to explain this divergence of later
sociology from his ideal He puts, it will be noticed,
the supremacy of the intelligence first among the
marks of progress. It goes with an increase in the
sympathetic instincts in our nature as compared
with the purely personal, but the intelligence comes
first as the agent and the index of progress. Now
intelligence is primarily and chiefly shown in
correct observation of the phenomena of our
existence and in so seeing their relations that we
are able to predict the future. This is of course the

function of science and, in the widest aspect of these relationships, of philosophy. It therefore follows that the primary work of a sociologist, according to Comte, will be to trace historically how this has taken place, and it is a signal confirmation of this reading of Comte's sociology that the type of research, directly inspired by him, is rather into the history of science than into that of social habits and institutions which has since his time formed the bulk of nominally sociological work. Paul Tannery, Emil Meyerson, George Sarton, the most distinguished workers in the former field, would all readily ascribe their initial impulse to Auguste Comte, and they rank as historians of science and not as sociologists, while, as we have seen, the nominal modern sociologists frequently turn their backs upon him.

Is not then the evolution of the human mind to be considered as a part—the leading part, as Comte would have claimed,—of sociology? It is a large question to which reference must be made more than once in subsequent chapters. Here it must be sufficient to point out two things about it; first, that Comte gave precedence to it as the fundamental law of his sociology; second, that with him it has a quality of inevitability which ill accords with the current pessimism and uncertainty of the day. The human mind has grown in the past and its growth is the supreme ascertainable law of our existence. Unless we postulate a reversal of this law, it will continue to grow hereafter. This conclusion, which would have seemed a tame commonplace a hundred years ago, is now sometimes attacked as facile optimism.

CHAPTER V

THE GROWTH OF MIND

THE classification which Comte adopts, and the order into which he divides the evolution of mankind, rests on the degree of scientific thinking which men had on the whole at that time attained. This is justified by the belief that abstract ideas are in the last analysis the determining factor in social action, and that man's superior intelligence is his distinguishing feature. But because it is distinguishing, it is by no means dominant at any time, and least of all in the imagined earliest stage in which he is struggling like other creatures to live and propagate and enjoy his life. He acts at first mainly by instinct, the habits ingrained in him by generations of awakening life in which his superior awareness and more adaptable bodily structure play a growing part. A life, however, in which a general theory of existence was dominating a society, still more one in which the individual could enjoy reflective contemplation for its own sake, must have been long in coming.

The first and most important general condition to be reached was one of practical common sense, an awareness of the actions necessary to secure a stable existence for the species, and Comte frequently insists on this as the basis for all later mental evolution. Science which later becomes abstract, is in essence "un simple prolongement du bon sens, de la raison publique, de la sagesse universelle."

Later thought and discoveries in the field of pre-history have done much to confirm this general view. At every step fresh links have been found between animal and human characters and genealogy. The "sagesse universelle" thus goes back and back till it loses itself in the emergence of life itself. On the other hand, all the remains which have been found of early men, give more prominence to their artistic qualities and afford little evidence of what they thought about the world around them. We classify these early civilizations —if one may use the word about them—by the style of their artefacts, their pottery, paintings and carving. What they thought about things or whether they could even talk in an articulate fashion, we can only guess. One knows in certain cases that they had some belief about the after existence of their dead, and this has given rise to one theory as to an "animistic" rather than the fetishistic origin of religion. But the fact remains that our solid knowledge is infinitesimal about the mental state of those unnumbered generations which must have filled the earlier æons of human life. On the capital point whether the given race of beings had attained an ordered general speech, being often in doubt, we are unable to take the first step in assigning them a philosophic view. For philosophy, logic and ordered science have been bound up throughout their course with the development of language. Often, as in Greek, the same word describes the whole. Logos is, Speech and Reason. There is therefore a marked contrast between the way in which the modern archæologist discusses primitive man and the conclusions Comte put forward, arguing philosophically and inferentially from the nature of abstract thinking and the way in which the young and savage men are now known to think. Art now bulks much more largely in our view both of the education of the young and the actual education of the human race, and the accepted opinion is much less confident and dogmatic as to how the earliest men framed their first thoughts as to the world in which they toiled. It is the largest, and so far the least cultivated, area in the history of the human mind.

Comte, from the analogy of the youthful mind

67

and from many examples of extant savage thought, imagined the primitive state of mind to be one in which all the objects which man encountered, seemed to be animated by a thinking mind and spirit like his own. He called this stage of thought "fetishism" borrowing the word from C. de Brosses, who wrote a book on the *Culte des Dieux Fétiches* in 1760. It is, of course, impossible here to discuss the theory or any of its rivals, but important to note its position in Comte's mind for he deduced from it the whole subsequent course of theological and even metaphysical thought. Fetishism is the first phase of the first stage of theology—of the famous three—theology, metaphysics and positivism—which give the fundamental law. Fetishism has also a further interest, for he returned later in life to a transformed and elevated type of it which bears much resemblance to the poetic thought familiar to us in writers like Wordsworth and George Meredith. No one acquainted with the latter can help comparing Meredith's adoration of the Earth, and frequent invocation of "Her" with the *"Grand Fétiche"* of Comte's later mysticism.

As to the primitive man, one may well believe that such imaginings played a large part in his poetry. The actual objects which surrounded him, were sometimes supposed to be alive; or to be tenanted by a spirit of the dead revisiting the earthly scene. But one would be very cautious to-day in classing under one simple formula all the thoughts that men living, during half a million to a million years, may have entertained about a world, the conditions of which we have yet carefully to explore. It is more important, for the comprehension of how thought gradually took solid and effectual shape, to consider that at every stage both of purely artistic, as well as practical work, man was learning the ABC of the language of Nature herself. Now this ABC which leads ultimately to sociology, gives in its simplest combinations the elements of mathematics. Counting and measuring are the first scientific processes to be done accurately and this was done at the dawn of abstract thought. Even animals and notably birds, have been proved capable of counting as far as some savages, and measuring which must be done unconsciously by birds in their flight and animals in the chase, becomes conscious and necessary in the most primitive civilization. The man measured when he stood up to make a painting on the wall or sat down to shape a garment or fashion a tool. In this matter, as in the beginnings of religion, one has learnt since Comte's day, to be both more

comprehensive and less definite in the assignments
of dates and sources. With all pre-history to draw
on, who will now confidently state that the
Egyptians invented geometry for the remeasuring
of the fields after the flooding of their river? Or
indeed that any one person or people invented any
one of the capital fundamental inventions which
have built up the world of men. Measuring,
weighing and counting must have gone on for
countless ages before the exquisite and meticulous
work which we now know from so many pre-
historic sites, long before the hey-day of Egyptian
civilization. And these artistic objects also involve
at least the raw material of what became later
other separate sciences; much more metallurgy than
we had suspected, and a careful study of animal and
vegetable forms. In one respect, however, recent
discoveries in the history of science confirm the
general view laid down by Comte in his survey of
the same field. He saw, as was said above, that
science, like art, religion and all the fundamental
manifestations of the human mind, was social in
origin, a *"prolongement,"* as he said, of the *"sagesse
publique."* But it does not take a definite form, is
not organized to become a spiritual force directing
the individual, until a separate order or class of men
arises to give their minds to it. Thus Egypt became

the teacher of the Greeks through her priests, and we now see that Babylonia had attained an even higher degree of mathematical skill, also through her priesthood attached to the throne. Here is the germ of science cultivated for its own sake, which must subsist side by side with science arising from practical work. Both developments are necessary to progress, and it is customary and useful to speak of the birth of science in the stricter sense of the word from the time when such special cultivation became possible. So far as the records tell us at present, this condition was first achieved in the two river-valleys of the Near East where ease of living made a leisured class possible. In a stricter sense, again, the birth of science has been referred to the Greeks, as they were the first to cultivate it as a free and disinterested activity of the mind, apart from the service of gods or monarchs whose necessities had prompted the earlier priests. In another sense, too, it is right to restrict the term to the Greeks, for they were the first known to us who introduced the idea of a general law or equation common to a number of particulars. Above all, with them the cultivation of the mind became a recognized aim, the noblest which man sufficiently qualified for it, could set before themselves as an object for life.

Recent discoveries of mathematical, and other scientific work among the Babylonians and Egyptians do not therefore appear to invalidate what Comte had pointed out about the unique contribution of the Greeks. When it is considered that the whole course of the conscious building up of the scientific and philosophic mind comes thus well within three thousand years, since the Greeks made their contact with the theocratic wisdom of the early priesthoods, it must appear as the greatest of known marvels, for the time is but a clock's tick, even in the span of man's life on earth. In Comte's view this course is taking us along the only line available for the understanding of the working of the universe in which we live. He discarded entirely any other source of information and did not hold that science itself gave, or could give, more than a changing, as he frequently said, a "relative" view of the facts. The view was relative to the state of man's mind and life at the time in which it was formed. Clearly therefore the thinking being—i.e., Humanity itself—becomes, within the limits of its being, supreme. There is no need to set up an altar or proclaim a worship. The historic fact itself is evidence enough. The growth of mind in the period of which we have knowledge is a guarantee, unless our conclusions are all baseless, that the growth will continue. The supreme known and growing thing, i.e., Humanity, or the human mind in evolution, subsumes into itself all the "laws," i.e., the proved regularities of the phenomena on which it is based and from which it has arisen.

Thus summed up, the universe might appear a repulsively abstract and bloodless thing; but it should be remembered that the "thinking," of which this is a rough general analysis, is only one aspect of the growth of mind which is the central fact in the universe. Men and all other sentient creatures have from the first been "thinking" in many other ways than that of the ordered thought which leads to science. There is the thought of the absent which forms what is commonly called "imagination"; there is the thought of the future which prompts to action and forms plans; there is a "thinking" closely allied to feeling, giving a passionate strength to what is being done at the moment. The sketch which is being given is not a psychological analysis of the whole mind, but merely of the type of thought which seeks and brings order into the phenomenal world, and, by establishing laws or uniformities, has had the most decisive effect in framing our lives. At the root of this type of thinking come the facts, or discovered laws, of size, position and number. These form the fundamental science of mathematics which is common to all phenomena, including those of the being which apprehends them. To the Greeks, who first elaborated them as a whole, they were so clearly universal and fundamental, that the very name, which is Greek, is equivalent to knowledge of every kind. As time went on, and more facts, and more complicated, were brought into the ambit of mathematical thought, the science which started first because it was the simplest, became actually the most complex and remote from our experience. This is one of the strangest, and yet most necessary, paradoxes in the growth of mind. But safety must be sought in this development, and in every other, by constant return to reality and the testing by results. That he was always ready to do so, would qualify Comte's philosophy for the title of "pragmatic," though the school of thinkers who use the name, are so much later than Comte. His whole method of approach to truth is on pragmatic lines, though he would have abstained from saying that there was *nothing more* than successful working to constitute a truth. Only this was obvious to him, that it is historically, i.e., by seeing how they arose, and how they justify themselves in action, that we can judge of the nature of the laws of thought. It was precisely in his own time, when the positive philosophy was being worked out, that the most signal proofs of the practical truth of mathematics were afforded to Western men. It was the age of Fourier, of Becquerel, of Poinsot and a host of others in France. The French were conducting a colossal work in describing mathematically the coast and soil of France and neighbouring lands. The English were devising practical means, by steam railways and electric cables, for linking up mankind.

Historically, the next science to mathematics was astronomy. It was indeed in its earlier form geometry applied to the heavens, though the movements of the bodies measured and their re-appearance in the same, or slightly altered, positions introduced from the first the element of prediction which Comte placed high, both as a test of science and for its practical value in ordering and pacifying the human mind. That astronomy did so with less cultivated peoples, was early observed by the Greeks themselves. The effect of the supremacy of the sun in religious worship, of eclipses in produc-ing panic fear in the minds of those who do not understand them, is a familiar fact on which we need not dwell. But there is one aspect of astronomical thought which is less familiar, though it is highly significant in this scheme of science leading to sociology. Not only are we a part of these revolving spheres, and the laws of their movements are therefore part of the laws of our own, but the very laws which describe them are part of our own mental history. They are a part of us as we of them.

After astronomy in the history of science came the foundations of physics. This turned to the qualities, the laws of change and movement in the parts or elements of the material world. When Thales as tradition goes, declared that "water" was the origin of all things, he was announcing a physical proposition. In this, however, the ancients achieved less of permanent value than they did in astronomy because the facts were less obvious to their unaided senses. There were guesses, as of the atoms of Democritus and Lucretius, and mathematical intuitions as of Archimedes and the laws of equilibrium. But the science tarried, partly because of the too great readiness of the Greeks to guess and their too little patience in observation; partly because they had not yet the mechanical instruments which made more accurate and minute observation possible. Comte is fully justified, however, in placing physics at this stage in the development and also in declaring that "experiment" is the characteristic method. Here the Greeks, with Archimedes, struck the keynote. His immortal experiment with the gold and silver crown will remain for all time the first and most significant. Again we see that the laws discovered apply just as much to the experimenter as to the body on which he is experimenting.

Chemistry which comes next in Comte's classification, and is now so closely interwoven with physics, cannot be exactly dated as a science. These early artists of Ur and Egypt must have known a great deal of what is commonly called chemistry. In the stricter sense, of a science with its proper nomenclature and its laws of combination, chemistry clearly belongs to the eighteenth century. It had just taken shape under Lavoisier when Comte was born. But as a stage in the growth, either of thought generally or of the thought of Comte, it was less important than the contemporary steps in the building up of biology. Here was the greater gap in the facts to be correlated and described: here was the broad and direct high road to the science of human life; and this step again was taken during the youth of Comte.

The material for a science of life had always

been ready to the eye and hand of man, as it is indeed to those of other animals. When did he begin to make a science of these facts? The answer given will depend upon the sense we attach to the word "science." At present, everyone would agree that it is a science, although it has attained nothing like the accuracy, or the number of accepted "laws," which we can point to in the sciences of the inanimate. At the other end of its history, few, if any, would hold that biology was a science in the time of Aristotle, in spite of his contributions to its study. Therefore, by common consent it has become a science somewhere between Aristotle and the present. This, which is one of the most important stages in the growth of mind will be dated by most students towards the end of the eighteenth century, when Comte found biology rendered scientific, firstly, by the great mechanical law which Harvey had introduced into physiology a hundred and fifty years before; still more by the all-embracing conception of a "consensus," not only within the living organism itself but between the organism and its environment or "milieu." This idea had become current about the turn of the century and has gained in strength ever since. Men like Professors J. S. Haldane or L. J. Henderson,[1]

[1] See his *Fitness of the Environment* and *Order of Nature*.

who encourage the fullest research into the bio-chemical factors which condition life, agree with Comte in holding that they can never furnish a complete explanation. This is to be found in some law of consensus or organization which seems to become more elusive and profound the further we trace it through its physical and chemical conditions. The recognition of a higher law for living things was to Comte the test of philosophic thinking in this sphere, and to deny it the capital instance of "materialism," or the explanation of the higher order of events in terms of the lower. When biology was founded, the longest step had been taken towards the institution of sociology as a science. It should be noticed that psychology on which contemporary thought would rest sociology more directly than on biology, was to Comte a great subdivision of biology itself. He avoided speaking of psychology as an independent science, owing to the aberrations of the "psychological school" of his own time who derived from Victor Cousin and based their conclusions on pure intro-spection. To Comte comparison was the sovereign method in psychology as in biology and he looked to biology as giving the guarantee for the possibility of a science of human life. If there is a science of living things, on what grounds can we exclude

79

man who is the highest of living things? We shall return more fully to this question in the next chapter; but, as we approach it, it may be well to indicate the *prima facie* reasons why man must be included;

In the first place, his nature includes, and rests on, all the laws of the lower sciences which have been already established.

In the second place, as a living being, he is part of the order which has been accepted as biological since the eighteenth century, and of which a "consensus" is the characteristic mark. In no member of the living order is this consensus so marked a feature as in the human organism and in the human race as a whole.

A third consideration remains, which has gained vastly in force since Comte's initiation of sociology a hundred years ago and now connects the science of man more strongly with the whole of biology than it could be connected then. This is the theory of descent with modification which became dominant in biology through the work of Darwin and is now held indisputably to connect mankind with the higher animals by community of blood and origin. Here the "historical method" which Comte claimed for sociology, finds a place also in the wider field of biology, though, as we pass in the next chapter more deeply into the human social order, we shall find a fresh difference arise as great, or perhaps greater, than that which separates the science of the living from that of the inanimate world.

CHAPTER VI

THE ADVENT OF SOCIOLOGY

THE last chapter brought us to the threshold of the greatest achievement in Comte's thought, that by which he will be known and judged so long as his name is remembered. The sudden inspiration of the word "Sociology" will secure that, as "biology" had become another fixed point in history, about thirty years before. Clearly, no one man ever does all the work represented by these turning points, and the business of the student who comes after, is to disentangle the mass of facts, so far as he may, and so far as it is profitable to do so, and assign his due share to the reputed founder, while estimating broadly the state of things as it existed before. In one sense there had been a sociology ever since men had begun to make and record observations about their own doings and thoughts. There is in this sense abundance of sociology in Egyptian papyri or the pages of Herodotus. But it is not sociology as we are to find it in Comte. It consists in those cases of interesting remarks connecting men's actions with their causes, but having no conscious bearing on the course of human history as a whole. "Life is given to the peaceful and death to the criminal," or "Men say that the Phœnicians were the cause of the difference which arose between the Persians and the Greeks," and so forth. With the progress of philosophy, and the more settled state of larger tracts of the earth's surface, wider views became current. One may date these most conveniently from the establishment of the Roman Empire, or, at the earliest, the preliminary attempt in the same direction by Alexander the Great. Universal ideas certainly appeared at those times, but they were not connected with the operation of natural causes on mankind, but were a sort of theophany—the god-like Alexander reviving the spirit of the Greek Achilles and making friends with the best of the world, or the divine Julius embodying the conquering genius of the Romans, and so on. In the Middle Ages, and down in fact to the end of the seventeenth century with Bossuet, the same way of philosophizing about history took on Christian language. The Catholic Church, succeeding to Rome, was the instrument in God's wisdom for bringing mankind together and promoting their happiness and peace. This is of course a definite

83

sociological theory, and was treated by Comte with much respect. Any such conspectus foreshadowed his own view, but differed from it by having a theological and not a positive or scientific basis. We may indeed, if we please, interprete the evidence, either of nature or of history, in theological terms, but the actual evidence is what we know of men's actions and their causation by natural events or the actions of other men. And, side by side, with these theological accounts came a series of what Comte called "metaphysical" explanations, from the Stoics down to his contemporary Hegel. There is no space here to give even the briefest sketch of these, if it had been worth while. Their common feature was to substitute for the idea of a divine agent some such conception as Nature, or the Spirit of the World or the Necessity of things, or Absolute Being realizing itself. Thinkers just before Comte had begun to look more closely into natural causes for the explanation of man's evolution, and, in particular, Montesquieu to whom Comte always refers as a leader in this line of thought, had traced the genesis of human societies largely to the influence of climate. It was left to Comte to look for the explanation in the nature of man himself, coming as the crowning manifestation of life as a whole.

84

Since Comte's day the idea of life as a continuous and developing thing has become more and more the dominant fact in the consciousness of thoughtful men. Many now look upon the whole Universe as a living thing, coming to flower and fruit again and again in series of organic beings such as have culminated on our planet in Man. Life to such a view would appear as an eternal thing. While Comte enters into no such distant speculations, it is interesting to note how his reading of mental evolution, as we know it on earth, would fit into such a wider scheme. We have been pressing back into the past since his time that line of life on earth which we are all now agreed must be continuous with that of man. In its earliest form we can distinguish two features which are as fundamental in our own nature as in the amœba or simplest organism of the primeval flood. On the one hand, is the consensus or tendency to act together and persist in life. On the other, is a constant and growing awareness of what surrounds the living thing. From the latter, which is the germ of consciousness, comes in due time all the activity, the creative power, the knowledge and aspiration which we recognize in other creatures and supremely in ourselves. Comte's analysis is useful and enlightening on the main aspects and turning-points in the later and relatively recent stages in this growth. All the earlier, and by far the larger, part of this process is veiled from our direct study. The latter portion, in ourselves and the animals most akin to us, is being revealed by comparative psychology, and Comte bases sociology upon the completed structure. "La présence," he tells us, "d'un être tel que l'homme implique tout l'ensemble des lois qui régissent notre monde." Man has arisen from them; he contains them in his own nature and in the last stage, of which Comte was the unquestioned herald, he begins to understand them.

The earliest awareness of the living thing was concerned entirely with its preservation and growth. But even so it must distinguish. The distinguishing act is involved in awareness. The simplest organism distinguishes between the sort of external material which sustains life and the sort which does not, between the type of living creature which is congenial and that which is harmful. Such awareness comes first and is fundamental. But gradually, amid this and arising from it, comes the more ordered and articulate awareness of which science is made. Number and distance are the first definite manifestations of the latter, and who can say at what point in the animal series they first appeared? We saw in the last chapter how from those simple perceptions mathematics arose, and that science therefore has its roots in the pre-human mind. Such inquiries belong to the sort of psychology which Comte advocated, while depre-cating that which tried to derive the laws of thought from introspection of the individual mind alone. In analysing the forms of thought, as Comte does in his classification based on history, he is merely following a method in the case of mental growth strictly analogous to that commonly applied in biology to animal and vegetable forms. The whole is continuous and is rightly subsumed under one conception of evolving life. But the individual types, say of reptile and bird, become so distinct that we study them as independent beings, of which the differences are often more striking than the common features which lie deep below the surface. Between the growth of animal types and the growth of mind there is, however, one profound and highly significant difference. The biological types have tended constantly to diverge. The forms of thought, though becoming more complicated, are always being more closely identified in principle and harmonized in general aim. Life, from its root in infinite time, has branched out more and more widely in all direc-tions. Thought, as soon as consciousness awoke,

87

tended always to unity. In our own day, for instance, the stars have found their way into the physicists' laboratory and physics and chemistry seem to join hands in the latest analysis of the atom. In Comte's view, the whole came to such unity as was possible in the constitution of sociology, which, being primarily the science of the collective mind, must by its very nature bring together all the preliminary sciences which had been created by that mind on its way to sociology. At each stage in the evolution of scientific thought some new principle and method came into play, experiment in physics, classification in chemistry, consensus and continuity in biology. Sociology embraces and may make use of all. But the last two steps, into the science of life with biology, and into that of the collective mind with sociology, are so specially important, and involve so much that seems subversive of the lower sciences, that it is necessary to dwell a little longer on them.

We have seen that biology was named, and became indisputably a science, at the end of the eighteenth century, just in time to give Comte his cue for its extension on a higher plane to the life of man. It is interesting to note that both the thinkers, Treviranus and Lamarck, who may claim the distinction of having at least named the science,

88

found its basis in the theory of "descent with modification." Treviranus seems to have been the first to put into words the idea which was to work so widely and profoundly a hundred years later. He wrote, "Protists, or zoophytes, are the primitive type from which all the organisms of the higher classes have arisen by gradual development."

Here we have the other fundamental link between the science of living things as a whole, and the science of man. Both, dealing with organisms, involve both a consensus in the being which the science describes, and a certain law of development, which in the broad sense of that term we may call "historical." In the contrasted phrase, which Comte made famous, there is a statical and a dynamic view of all living things. We shall see, as we proceed, that one, perhaps the most profound, of the differentiæ of the human collective organism, compared with less-developed beings, is the growing superiority of this dynamic over the static aspect. But the preliminary and most important fact is, that sociology rises out of biology, and as a science could not have come into existence without it. Had there been no Lamarck, there had been no Comte.

In considering more carefully what is involved in this last great step in Comte's hierarchy of the

sciences, it is no help to say that in the human
sciences man is thinking about himself, and that
this makes him a thing apart. He is not apart, and
cannot make himself so. All the lower creation is
summed up in him, and makes his nature, plus
something else. It is just that something else of
which we are in search. No doubt all the higher
animals—those, i.e., with a developed nervous and
cranial system like our own,—also think something about themselves and the world around them.
This is what consciousness means, and we cannot
make consciousness the dividing gulf which is
implied in most forms of metaphysics, because we
have already admitted that there is a science of
biology, including the higher animals and with
ascertainable laws of its own. We must admit the
kinship, even the large community, with the
higher animals, and seek further to find the real
differentiæ. Let us start with our sense of kinship,
let us say with the dog. This is a very real thing,
involving a community not only of many physical
features, but of much also in the sphere of feeling
and thought. It is quite a different thing from that
sense of oneness which some poets feel in presence
of a mountain or a stream. Yet we know also
that there is a distinctive something, which may be
analysed and described, which we as men possess,

and into which the dog cannot enter, much as we may love him and he us. What is this?

In the first place, it is obviously a mental difference. Considered merely as an animal, and with detailed differences as to size and position of organs, the dog and the man function physiologically alike. Their nervous, muscular, respiratory, alimentary and reproductive systems are similar. If we classified on this basis, we should only be classifying in the same way as we distinguish dogs from monkeys, horses or any other vertebrates. Knowing that there is something more fundamental, we are driven to find it elsewhere, and it must be found in the mental, or, in the most general sense of the word, in the spiritual, sphere. But here again we are driven to seek further, because mentally the dog has many,—some would say most—basic features in common with us. His senses are similar; he remembers many things, especially places and persons, often better than we do; he is attached, he fights, he has likes and dislikes much as we have, and he directs his actions in simple cases to satisfy his needs in much the same way. The differentiæ to be sought must therefore be things larger, higher or more remote than these. Comte thought, and in this he has the common sense of mankind with him, that the difference had become a funda-

AUGUSTE COMTE

mental thing by a process of small changes which
have taken place in time, though not mainly in
the historic time of which we have record. He
found the mental difference, as most men would
find it, in three or four great characteristics which
we can easily apprehend, and of which we can
trace the growth partly in historic, still more in
pre-historic ages.

Those who hold this view have to face one
difficult, but quite inevitable, problem. At a
certain point in the process there comes a moment
when a difference in degree becomes a difference
in kind, when Man is made and is no longer
merely an animal. Because in spite of all the kinship which we admit between ourselves and them,
no one thinks that sociology, or the human sciences
generally, apply to animals as well as men. There
is kinship and yet a difference in kind. We cannot
explain the change but can illustrate it from many
other phenomena of life. From an undifferentiated
egg, comes a being complete in its proper species,
but no one can fix exactly the point at which the
embryo became the female child. We must believe
the same about all slowly growing things and be
ready to accept the infant man, the nation or
Humanity itself when they are formed.

The mind in man, therefore, which contains his

differentia, is similar to, or even identical with, the animal's in its earliest stage, but becomes so far richer and more powerful in its human stage that we then acknowledge a difference in kind. The two points in this mental growth on which Comte laid most stress, were its social and its historical character. Man's mind, like everything which he possesses which is human, is at the same time and *ipso facto*, social. By a progressive enrichment in the course of evolution man's mind, being social, also acquires a superiority and power over the individual of which we see only the faintest adumbration in other animal species. Many act, as it seems, blindly in the interest of the herd or swarm, but there is no instance which we can detect, of a social conscience or being among them, accumulating the experience of the past and using it freely to guide and alter their present conduct. If such a process has ever taken place, the results are now stereotyped and we can see no further change. The historical process, which in the animal becomes a corporeal or instinctive thing, becomes in man an enrichment and enlargement of the mind. It is the difference in the working of history, or the time-factor, in the two cases which produces the final difference in kind.

So far the argument will be generally admitted.

93

The common sense of mankind sees at once that it is by virtue of his mind that man has risen above the beasts and is shaping his environment. But when Comte asks us to see this mental development in the one straight line of science which he is prepared to map out for us in neat consecutive periods, ending in a millennium after which no substantial change need be expected, at once our critical instinct is awake. Does this orthogenic line really describe and embrace all that matters in the growth of mind? Is it truly drawn so as to come to its climax so aptly with the work of Comte? Does the sequel since his death bear out the judgment on which it was based? Clearly some sort of answer must be offered to such far-reaching questions, and much of it must be postponed till we come to deal with the story of sociology since the days of the founder. On one point, however, the first, something should be said here, while we are discussing the scheme as it took shape in the founder's mind. Why should science enjoy such a prerogative position among the manifestations of the human mind? Men have been doing and thinking a million other things while science has been growing. They have founded states and written poetry. They have portrayed in painting and the plastic arts their impressions of the outer world. They have propagated their own and other species in a thousand types, which were unknown when science began. All this is both true and weighty and must be allowed for in a complete picture of human progress. The material of sociology has indeed become embarrassingly richer in the course of time. But there is also something decisive to be said for the prerogative position of science as Comte described it. The evolution of science is the course taken by the mind in its most abstract, most purely mental and most clearly progressive direction. On that line of progress, we have the most authentic and indubitable records. It is the form of mental action which is most directly and obviously justified in action, and, more than any other, it is common without distinction to all parts of mankind. These are strong reasons for using it as the yard-stick for computation, even though—which is also true—it is at no time the main interest of the race. Comte, it must be held, did a great service to clearness and solidity of thought in putting this line of evolution in this prominent place.

The last chapter gave a sketch of the main pre-liminary stages. Thoughts about number and distance went on accumulating, and being corre-lated, until at last they were viewed as one coherent

whole. This whole was then used as the sub-
structure of another building; and so with the
rest. This is the general scheme and the rising of
sociology to crown the whole was quite similar.
The facts, which took their place as sociology when
it was founded, had been massing themselves since
history began. The Greeks had been the greatest
accumulators and had done pioneer work in draw-
ing early schemes for seeing the facts in their
connexions. But a comprehensive view was not
possible until the idea of a general forward movement, common to all mankind, had taken possession of the minds of thinking men. This came after
the Christian era and was largely conditioned by it.
After the general establishment of Christianity in
the West, ideas of kindred scope became more and
more common in philosophic minds, and tended
more and more to rest on natural rather than
assumed or *a priori* principles. Then came the
conception of a growing spiritual force, arising
from men's own minds, though resting on and
conditioned by the laws of physical nature and of
life. This was the historic genesis, both of sociology and of the conception of Humanity which is
inseparable from it. The time was ripe, and it fell
to Comte to give the first formulation of the
master-thoughts.

Whatever may be the final judgment on this formulation, the master-thoughts must persist because they describe a reality which was coming into being at the time in which they were formed. All must agree, at least as to the possibility of a collective human spiritual force, who see in a nation anything beyond the individuals who compose it, or in any social aggregate anything beyond its constituent atoms.

A fervid advocate of the League of Nations, was lamenting lately, with good apparent reason, the absence of an *Anima Societatis* in the world to-day. He bore witness in his own words to the existence of the very thing which he desired, for he, and many others, feel its reality, and what they truly mean is that they do not see it as active around them as they would wish. But it is there, and will grow, if there is any truth in the whole course of human thought which has brought sociology to birth. Its framework is the order of the sciences, but it has substance also in the feelings which unite mankind and in the ideals for the future which men conceive and into which they throw their energies of action. There is too a collective vision, compounded of the myriad thoughts which individual seers have added to the common treasure in the past. The new force works more

97

slowly than we would have it do, because, besides the strength of inertia and of selfish habits long ingrained, the facts of this highest of the sciences are incomparably more complex than those of any other. But with this complexity comes a greater power of modification. This was the last and most hopeful of the signs which Comte discerned to mark the phenomena of human action. We can modify, though we must modify according to the laws which predict the effects of such actions. We cannot modify the courses of the stars but the courses of human action are accessible to influence, and each new thought, if conformable to the general trend of human life, strengthens the tendency and grows by exercise.

This, it will be seen, is a historical view. It involves a belief that, in the region of life, and within the limits of our knowledge, we can trace a progressive development in time. This is true of all living things, but, with regard to mankind the development goes further and becomes in time different in kind as well as in degree, owing to the fact that the mind of man has acquired a consciousness of the past and uses that consciousness for its own further expansion. Comte's analysis deals with that growth of mind from one limited but, as he holds, dominant, aspect and he offers us a sketch which is unmistakable in its outlines and can be tested by reference to the historical facts which it professes to summarize, to connect and so far to explain. In Sociology he draws both his method and his supreme authority from history. He has a right to appeal to his own Cæsar, who happens to be acknowledged also by the leading thinkers, both of his age and of our own.

CHAPTER VII

THE HISTORICAL CONTENT

WE have now seen how Comte conceived of
Sociology as arising from the preliminary
sciences by a regular historical process, and how
the science of man's collective existence rests on
and comprises, all the other sciences. It is now time
to consider what he offered as the content of
that highest science itself. It must be, in accordance
with the principles already laid down, an ordered
conspectus of human history since the time when
we can speak of man as a distinct species, differing
in kind from the lower animals. Sociology thus
becomes, not exactly a philosophy of history, for
that seems to imply the principles directing our
conspectus rather than the conspectus itself, but
certainly, history philosophically considered.
Clearly, this is an immense and a constantly
growing mass of knowledge. Even for any one
who accepted Comte's reading of the past as true
when written, it could not be regarded as a final
account, partly because new events are constantly

happening which both add to the facts to be explained and also throw fresh light on those which have already occurred, partly because the records of the past are being constantly enlarged by fresh discoveries; and this has happened with unexampled rapidity since Comte's day. Reviewing it now, therefore, we shall be principally concerned with the validity of the leading ideas on which he worked and the brilliance of the insight which he shows in applying these ideas here and there to the facts on which he happens to touch. Such a review is well worth while even for a student who starts with a minimum of sympathy for the method employed, who may perhaps think that there is no such thing as a philosophy of history, or that, if there were, it would be quite unlike the philosophy of Comte. For the purpose of such a review, Miss Martineau's third volume[1] would probably be found sufficient. She did her work with great care and enthusiasm and it was accepted and recommended by the philosopher himself. The style of the original is highly involved and difficult.

The main ideas and the inspiration of Comte's sketch are its most important features, though the

---

[1] *The Positive Philosophy of Auguste Comte.* Freely translated and condensed by Harriet Martineau. 3 vols. Bell and Sons.

frequent illustrations from particular persons and
events are apt and striking. It will be remembered
that the root-idea is that human history consists
essentially in the growth of mind. Now the mind,
as judged by science, is similar in its methods and
results, whatever the race or local habitat of the
thinker. The sketch, therefore, must be orthogenic,
—one, in its main course and direction. There
are local variations in abundance, and these are
matter for descriptive history or sociology. But
the laws we are seeking belong to the main trunk,
the collective progress of mankind conceived as
one. We must look for them in the leading
branch of the race, and, judging always by the
growth of proved and ordered knowledge, there
has never been any question where this was to
be found. It is in what we now call "Western
Civilization," though, when we trace it back-
wards, we find that it has its roots and confluents
in many sections of mankind besides the Western.
It is in fact, by origin as well as destination,
universal. This main stream, however, within
historic time became confined mainly to the
countries surrounding the Mediterranean Sea. To
these therefore Comte devotes his attention.

The other leading idea—still more dominant
indeed over the whole process of his thought—

is that the progress to be analysed is a continuous and general fact. No doubt there are local setbacks as well as local variations, but "it must be evident that, in spite of unfavourable circumstances, the æsthetic, like all the other faculties of Man, are in a condition of continuous development."

Now, as this is the capital doctrine of the whole sketch and is also the one most disputed at the present day, it is necessary to state it a little more fully. No doubt the continued progress of mankind depends to a large extent on men's own efforts, and in this sense Comte would not say that the law was as "inevitable" as the movements of the planets. But when we take the historic point of view and consider the past as a fact, we are, he would say, as much entitled to regard progress as a certain and accomplished thing as any other movement of which we have traced the laws. Man has progressed, and is still progressing, in spite of all the breaks and falls. He finds the explanation in the growth of his mind, and, as that was manifestly proceeding at a still greater pace in his own time, he concludes that progress in the future is as certain and probably more rapid than in the past. His belief, no doubt, has been proved in the century since he wrote to be in certain points much too optimistic. This aspect of the matter must be dealt with in a later chapter. But it is essential to the understanding of the sketch of the past as a whole, which he presents, to grasp that he regards the past as an advance and a preparation for a much better state of which he has the ideal already laid up in his mind.

Following up these two main threads of his thought it is not difficult to reach the others. The thought of mankind has been in a state of continued change and development in time. But throughout, at least in historic time, man has been living in ordered societies, which imply a government and some control of passions and instincts which do not in their early state make for peace and co-operation. The two essential factors needed to secure the order, from which human progress is born, are government and religion, the latter being always the supreme necessity for the most effective conduct of life. As it is written clearly in history that the progress of thought has constantly disintegrated religious beliefs in the past, how is this needed guidance of mind and life to be secured in future? In Comte's time, and just before, the traditional beliefs of Christianity, still the acknowledged religion of the West, were discredited and discarded by science more widely than they had ever been before. Yet in his view religion was essential for holding society together and directing life. The two must somehow be combined and in this attempted combination Comte reaches the foundations of his polity for the future. Science had been growing and, as he saw it, displacing religious belief. Religion was proved by history to be the dominant condition of social union and effective life. Therefore in the future, which will follow the past, religion must be based on science.

Now the growth of thought which has given us science, is itself subject to a law of development which Comte often described as his capital discovery. This was the "law of the three stages," most discussed of all his particular theories. It may be found in a less sharply articulated form in Turgot's essays, though it does not appear that Comte had any knowledge of this, when he first propounded it himself. The theory is that man began his explanation of the world by imagining beings behind phenomena animated by thoughts and powers of action similar to his own. Thus the river flowed and the thunder roared just as men did with their own organs. This first stage of thought was what we now term "theological" and it had its own subdivisions. In the earliest of all, which Comte termed "fetishism," every object had a separate soul and men worshipped the particular stone or tree. In course of time these little divinities were merged into greater and we have the stage of "polytheism" when numerous gods were conceived of in control of whole departments of nature. This stage is best known to us in the religion of Greece and Rome, where Sky, Ocean, Earth, Birth, Harvest and Death are, with a host of other deities, worshipped as the most powerful supernatural forces. The second of the three great stages arrived gradually and sporadically as the critical mind began to question the reality of these beings and substituted for them spirits or abstract principles such as Nature or Fate. Clearly there was no sharp dividing line when all the beings of one order were abandoned for conceptions of another kind. A process of change was going on all the time and one order of events was being explained in one way while another had advanced into a more abstract stage. All were in fact advancing into the final or positive stage when men are satisfied with describing, arranging and connecting the phenomena which they observe and are content to leave the earlier creatures of their imagination to the field of fancy from which they sprang. The intermediate stage in which men were criticizing and dehumanizing the beings of their fancy, Comte generally termed the "metaphysical" stage, and it is this special use of the word "metaphysics" which often confuses a reader who has in mind the other commoner and more literal uses of the word from Aristotle downwards. In Comte's current usage, coloured by his special theory, it means a thinker, or a school of thinkers, who base their conclusions on illicit assumptions going beyond or behind the facts.

It should be noticed that this law of mental development through the three stages[1] has its counterpart or concrete illustration in the order and classification of the sciences themselves. Each order of phenomena gains its science, i.e., attains its positive stage, according to the simplicity and universality of its facts. Mathematics coming first in this sequence may be said never to have had a theological stage. There never was a god of number or of weight. The more complex and special the

[1] The best criticism of this suggested "law" to be found in English is that by the late Prof. L. T. Hobhouse in *The Sociological Review* for July, 1908. It amounts to saying that it is true that there is generally an early "fictitious" account of things to be explained, that this is followed by a "dialectical" stage in which argument is used for criticism and destruction, and that the final stage, which Comte described as "positive" is really the constant correction of our conceptions by reference to an experience becoming more and more complete.

phenomena are, the longer a theological or meta-physical explanation lingers among them. The mysterious weather still has its divine agencies all over the world, and, most mysterious of all, the acts of living things are to the last attributed to some supernatural force. Thus it came about that mathematics, physics, biology became positive sciences in that order.

The next chapter is to give some idea of the future State, as Comte conceived it, when the scientific or positive spirit is supreme. But it is right here to give a few illustrations drawn from his sketch of the past which show how he attempted to interpret what we actually know of these periods, in the light of the intellectual evolution which he regarded as the master-key. It will be seen at once how stupendous was the task proposed, nothing less than re-reading the whole story of mankind from a new, abstractly sound but concretely too schematic or formal, point of view. One may hold—as does the present writer—that the general attitude is the ideal interpretation to aim at, while recognizing constantly that fresh knowledge, or a more balanced judgment, would modify what we find in the author. Such correction and re-writing are impossible in this place; it is more to the purpose to dwell for a little on some of the points where light is clearly thrown by the application of his method.

It is true, instructive and stimulating throughout to note, as Comte does, that the various stages of man's thought have brought their appropriate and permanent contributions to his welfare and progress. Each stage, as he reads it, settles down to a system of life and government which is suitable to its conditions, and what he calls the "fetishistic" stage, which is far the longest in the existence of the race, brought the greatest boons of all. He shows how, during that time, partly by the use of his practical energy and wits, partly also by the affectionate and reverential spirit developed by his religious feelings, man laid the foundations of all the arts of life. The early belief in the power of external agents behind phenomena gave men the needed courage to proceed. A growing kindliness and patience are testified by the taming of all the lower animals which have ever been tamed. A keen imagination and a religious attitude towards other creatures and the external world are brilliantly demonstrated by the works of art which remain. These are now known in much greater abundance than they were in Comte's day and give still more force to his remark, "that the manifestation of some interest in the fine arts will ever be the commonest symptom of the birth of the spiritual life."

He traces the chief means of passing from the fetishistic to the polytheistic stage to astrolatry or star-worship. "There is a character of generality about the stars which fits them to be common fetiches." "Their superior generality and inaccessible position were reasons . . . why the adoration of them . . . determined the formation of an organized worship and a priesthood, and the advent of astrolatry was thus not only a symptom but a powerful means of progress in its day." It gave stability to the populations who lived under the ægis of the distant, dignified and slowly and regularly moving deities; and their priesthoods became the first systematic students and repositories of science.

The illustration is an excellent example of the value and the limitations of Comte's method. He puts into prominence an undoubted cause of human development which is commonly overlooked by the historians of political, social and economic facts, and that he, perchance in this or other cases, may attach undue importance to it, is a fault in the right direction, a certain redress of the balance which is habitually overweighted on the other side.

The treatment naturally becomes fuller as we pass from the dim fetishistic ages to the daylight of Greece and Rome. These represent, as types of "military polytheism," the successful effort of the more rapidly advancing portions of mankind to throw off the yoke of the star-worshipping theocracies which had lived so long and done so much for civilization in the valleys of the Euphrates and the Nile. They had by that time become effete and oppressive, as the contact of Greeks and Persians proclaimed for ever to the world. This military activity was politically barren among the Greeks, though it performed the special service of rescuing from theocratic influences that "little nucleus of freethinkers who were in some sort charged with the intellectual destinies of our race." But for the fine arts and science the Greeks did work of supreme and permanent value. In the fine arts their work follows more directly on the achievement of the fetishists and theocrats who had preceded them; in science we owe to them the first definite fruits of the positive spirit. These were naturally won in the field of mathematics, which form the necessary origin, from their simplicity, generality and abstract character, of rational positivism. Comte notes how the early sages or philosophers of Greece, like their sacer-

dotal precursors, cultivated all parts of the intellectual domain at once, but that soon that great
division arose which furnished the basis of our
scientific development. "Men of science properly
so called began to appear as a separate class from
the philosophers at the memorable epoch distinguished by the foundation of the museum of
Alexandria." At that period, in the inception of
science, specialism was needed and involved no
political disadvantages. Our modern need is of
new generalities.

It is striking and seems paradoxical that Comte,
whose theory of history elevates the growth of
mind to the place of highest guide and test, yet
speaks so much more warmly of the work of
Rome than of Greece, and of the medieval period
than of either. The explanation is to be found
in the fact that the "mind" of which he thinks,
is always the collective, social mind, and that for a
mind, however ingenious, which spun its webs to
catch a prey for itself, he had nothing but repro-
bation at any period. Thus Alcibiades the typical,
brilliant, unscrupulous Greek would go down
with Napoleon to the lowest circle of Dante's
Hell. Both Greece and Rome were, in his scheme,
the representatives of the "military polytheism"
whose function in the ages was to lead the way

to a form of belief and government which could unite the world. This must be monotheism in belief, and, at that time, empire in government. Both peoples were equally given to fighting, but, whereas the geographical and personal conditions in Greece prevented their forming a large united state, the Romans were admirably adapted in both respects. Hence to them must go the palm of final success. Their absorption in this all-important task withdrew their minds from the prosecution of abstract science in which the Greeks did their most signal work. But the building up of science belongs to all mankind. The priesthoods of theocracy had led the way; Alexandria took it up when the ancient world began to be settled as a whole; and the Middle Ages, so unjustly despised as "Dark Ages" by modern anti-Catholic revolutionaries, actually contributed greatly to the growth of science as they did to all the other essential factors in the permanent state of the future.

He notes—what is indeed obvious—that the polytheism of the Greeks offered the most favourable field for the expansion of an art which became more human in its idealization as its gods became humanized. But his loudest and least qualified praises are given to the qualities of tenacity, patriotism and legality which enabled the Romans, in their uncorrupted period, to build up the Western world. There was a growing humanity among them which bore fruit both in private and public morals. "The introduction of family names, unknown to Greece, is a sufficient testimony to the growth of the domestic spirit." Social morals also were in a rising state, in spite of their savage games and the brutality of their slave system. The latter was gradually softened in the legislation of the empire and there was always a tendency to treat the vanquished in such a way as led to the doctrine of universal charity soon to be proposed by a monotheistic church.

And so we come to the millennium of the Catholic Church, on which Comte's eulogistic judgment has been most disputed by his critics, and is in least accord with the revolutionary spirit of the times in which he wrote or of those which have succeeded him.

Neither criticism nor defence will be attempted here, but a simple statement of those features in the times and system which seemed to Comte to justify the judgment which he passed. He would probably have put first that quality of continuity in history, the bringing together of various strains in human development, which belongs conspicuously to Catholicism and cannot be said to have appeared before Christian times in the world. "If we consider the filiation which connected Catholicism, on the one hand, with the Roman and on the other with the Greek regime, and even through Judaism with the most ancient theocracies; and again if we remember its continuous intervention in all great human affairs, we shall see that from the time of its full maturity under the great Hildebrand, the history of the Church was a kind of fundamental history of humanity, in its social aspect." This passage strikes also the second note in the Catholic system on which Comte returns again and again for favourable comment. Being a system based on the social aspect of life its very *raison d'être* is the elevation of the moral side of life over all the others. No system had done this before anywhere in the world, with the possible exception of Buddhism which was for the most part a quietist system for personal guidance rather than a rule of State. But, formally at least, the Christian Church made the maxims of its Founder the rule of life, both publicly and privately, and these unquestionably were based on the love of one's fellow-men, as being children of a common Father. Comte passes lightly over the grave and frequent breaches of these principles in Christian practice and thereby of course lays himself open

to damaging attack. But he persists in holding that
the public profession of the principles and their
enforcement, however imperfect, by an organized
body of men covering a far wider area than the
empire which preceded them, must have had in-
calculable effect in the direction desired. It was
indeed to him the prime cause of the moral
renovation of the Western world on which our
present virtues and stability are based. He carries
out the explanation into the particular changes
which belong to the medieval period. The
gradual transformation of slaves first into serfs
and then into free labourers he connects with the
spread of Christian doctrine and feeling. Whereas
later historians would give first place to economic
causes, while allowing a certain force to religion,
Comte would reverse the order and put religion
first; quoting the "famous bull of Alexander III
on the general abolition of slavery in Christendom
as a systematic sanction, rather late, of a custom
which had been extending for centuries. From the
sixth century on temporal chiefs who were under
the fresh influences of Christianity, had conferred
personal freedom sometimes on the inhabitants of
a considerable district. . . . The influence which
this wrought, was not of morality alone. The
morality was enforced by the persevering action

116

of a priesthood which was opposed to the institution of caste and open to be recruited from every social class, and which relied mainly for the permanence of its organization on the labouring classes whose rise it therefore constantly favoured."

The moral influence worked side by side with the economic, industrial and scientific; but in Comte's view must always be given first place. The total result was, in his view, the greatest revolution ever accomplished on earth. It has given us the mass of industrious, hard-working, free citizens of Western Europe, who, in its later extensions to America and other European colonies, now form the backbone of the human organism. Who, he asks, in his wildest dreams would have anticipated this result, if he had surveyed the world at the time of the slave farms of later Rome, or its depopulation under the wars of the barbarians? The miracle has been performed by a religious faith based on love and carried out by a well-organized body of apostles.

A similar line of argument explains the rise of the status of women in Christian times. It was connected in Comte's view with the definite assignment of women to the domestic sphere. That being from the moral point of view the most important, it was the highest distinction which

117

could be given to women. It was sanctified by
the worship of the supreme woman, the mother
of the divine child, and it was defended by the
indissolubility of marriage. His doctrine here takes
us on into the sphere of a polity for the future, but
its connexion with his reading of the Middle Ages
is obvious enough. Nor would there be much
dispute as to the historical truth of the judgment
on this subject. Whatever one's views on the
permanent relation of the sexes, the Catholic
millennium led to a vastly enhanced valuation of
women and a transformation of men's conceptions
of marriage and married love.

One more leading point on which Comte often
insists in treating of the Middle Ages, should be
mentioned here, for it is highly characteristic of
his general method. He inclines constantly to
make the principles he discovers by sociological
analysis, into matter for concrete institutions and
canons for permanent action in the future. In this
case he finds that in the medieval order a distinction was made between the "temporal" and
"spiritual" aspects of government which had
never been recognized under the military poly-
theisms of Greece and Rome. Such a distinction
was in fact alien to the very idea of a theocracy
which combined all authority in one person or one

governing body, and Greece and Rome had not in this respect separated their practice from that of the more ancient polities which they succeeded. Kings, Archons or Basileis had sacred as well as civil and military functions. With the advent of the Christian Church this was necessarily altered, for the Church grew up outside the State and was only gradually tolerated and finally recognized by the rulers of the State, who derived their authority from other sources. This purely historical causation assumed in Comte's eyes, and those of other apologists of the Catholic regime, all the weight of a deliberate division of functions, carried out on philosophical principles. That there is a real distinction between matters resting on personal and religious conviction, and those more general matters which affect the safety and welfare of all and must be controlled by the temporal arm, is of course a far-reaching and useful canon. Comte does well to point it out, and modern States have striven with more or less honesty and success to carry it out. On the other hand, it is equally clear that there is a mass—possibly the greater part—of man's actions in which a divided allegiance and control are inevitable. Marriage, education and the host of questions concerned with public morality, must interest both the spiritual organs

and authorities in any country and also the
temporal authorities who have to preserve the
public order. No such sharp distinction can be
drawn as Comte suggests, and his treatment of
the matter is similar to the sharp schematizing
which we have noticed in the "law of the three
stages" and elsewhere.

But as we are looking throughout rather for
the sound ideas which are to be found in his
thought than for the numerous and obvious points
which invite criticism, it should be noted that his
praise of the division of the powers in the Middle
Ages, and his advocacy of it in his future polity,
arise, like the rest of his favourable judgment of the
Catholic régime, from his passionate concern for
the supremacy of the moral interests of mankind.
He was as truly a "morality-intoxicated," as
Spinoza was a "God-intoxicated," man. Morality
was to be supreme in art, science and politics,
especially the politics of international relations.
Because, as he thought, the actions of the temporal
rulers of any country, and at any time, were
bound to be largely governed by considerations
of expediency, he welcomed an independent voice
which would speak for the claims of the general
conscience. He found an adumbration of this in
the Church of the Middle Ages, and planned a

more perfect form for the same organ in the Spiritual Power of the future.

After the break-up of the medieval order in the fifteenth and sixteenth century, Comte's sketch of the rise of the modern world follows two channels. Interspersed with a number of remarks—often just and penetrating—on particular subjects and countries in modern Europe, there run two continuous threads through the latter portion of his sociological sketch. One is the action of what he commonly calls the negative or critical spirit, which found its culmination in such men as Rousseau at the time of the French Revolution. This spirit was steadily undermining the old order as represented by the Catholic Church. The other, proceeding side by side with it, was the growth of positive science, of which the great synthesis of Newton was the first conspicuous triumph. It promised by the end of the eighteenth century to sweep all thought and life into its circle. It will be well in another chapter to consider how Comte viewed this in relation to the whole question of man's welfare and his future. How does the growth of mind fit in with the growth of man?

CHAPTER VIII

THE IDEAL OF PEACE

ANYONE who follows Comte's sociological exposition of history, sketched in the last chapter, will be most struck by the serene confidence with which he moves on to the goal. There are none of the hesitating hopes which fill the minds of the most hopeful in our own days. Are we to say that he regarded the human millennium as an inevitable thing? In what sense can we regard any human event as inevitable, when subject to so many external chances and to the wayward wills of human beings? What are the main characteristics of the millennium which he foresaw, and, above all, what are the grounds of secure inference on which he rested? These are all questions of the deepest moment to thinkers at the present day, when it is only too evident that Comte's forecast has not been fulfilled in the exact way, or at the early moment, of his own vision.

It will be best to take first the main outlines of his forecast and then to consider the grounds on which he based it. What has happened in later and contemporary events, may be best treated in another chapter.

There can be no doubt in the mind of any fair-minded reader, who surveys his treatment as a whole, that the three main features which filled most space in his mind were science, industry and peace. He was convinced that the human race, using its own efforts but aided by the laws of nature which men must study and obey, could reach a state of universal peace and happiness to which we need not put any ascertainable limit. He saw this goal being reached gradually in history by many complicated steps, governed by a law of progression based ultimately on the growth of the scientific mind. It is true and obvious that this growth kept pushing into the background the fictitious, or theological, explanations of events which the imagination of men had been constantly weaving, and gaining thereby, courage and stability and happiness. But he is insistent that these explanations, though they may be disproved in the particular case, can never be disproved *in toto* because the mind which makes them cannot go behind phenomena, and there may be forces or causes of quite another order of which we can have no conception at all. It was a favourite saying of

123

his that the "atheist is the most irrational of all theologians," because, while undertaking to speak of such things, he begins by denying the very things of which he is speaking. His own attitude was to leave that order of assumed questions alone, and address the mind solely to that way of thinking which had been proved by history to lead to fruitful results. But for those who continued either to entertain traditional beliefs or frame new ones he had no hostility, provided only that they were willing to co-operate in the great common work of establishing the human ideal State. True, this State involves the use of the scientific mind but many men have done this in the most fruitful way while retaining in another compartment ideas which they regarded as religious and drew from sources not at all scientific. Sir Isaac Newton, the greatest founder of scientific syntheses, is a conspicuous example of this, for he studied the prophecies of Daniel at one time with a zeal equal to his study of the celestial universe and left behind him works on the *History of Creation*, *Paradoxical Questions Regarding Athanasius*, and many more. Comte, in later life, when his own ideal polity was framed, addressed letters both to the Pope and the Head of the Eastern Church, soliciting their help.

But we are here considering, not the steps which he took later for the propaganda of his doctrine, but the scientific basis on which he founded it. He did not preach peace, unity and industry to be gained by science, because the world was given up to other things and needed a refuge from its troubles. That was the spirit of the early Christian preachers who urged their hearers to escape from the evils of the present and the wrath to come. Comte's gospel, which in the eyes of sympathizers, has often seemed to mark a similar turning-point in history, directed men's minds to what had already been accomplished and asked them to consider the real significance of the events. The human world had become, by a process which we can trace in history, a place essentially transformed in structure and spirit. What is needed is that we should acquaint ourselves fully with what has happened and what has brought it about. Then, in the light of this knowledge and a newly in-formed and conscious will, we can advance to redress remaining weaknesses and make further conquests, on an extension of the same lines.

George Eliot, as we know, invented the word "meliorism," but Comte, to whom she owed so much, undoubtedly gave the idea a form and substance which it had never possessed before.

We noted in the last chapter the greatness of the social revolution in the Middle Ages which Comte ascribed mainly to the operation of the Christian spirit, and, above all, to the influence of the organized clergy drawn indifferently from all classes. He laid great stress on the fact that even serfdom was no bar to a man rising to the highest place in the Church, as in the case of Adrian IV, a Hertfordshire peasant, who was one of those Popes who asserted most successfully the prestige of his office. He held also—a doubtful judgment—that fighting in the Middle Ages was passing from the aggressive to the defensive stage. In this we have probably an example of his excessive tendency to orderly scheming of the facts, but on the main issue there can be no difference of opinion. At the end of the Middle Ages, when the serfs were free and industrial communities had arisen all over the West, "the greatest of temporal revolutions ever experienced by mankind had been accomplished." The wars which followed in the seventeenth and eighteenth centuries (after the Thirty Years War), engaged but a small part of the population and were fought by small and mostly professional armies. The mass of the population had by that time settled down into its normal state of peaceful industry which still persists in spite of the great upheaval 1914–18. "By this vast regeneration," says Comte, "the race closed its preliminary period and entered upon its definitive state in regard to practical life, which was henceforth brought into agreement with our general nature; for a life of labour is, when become habitual, the fittest to develop all our chief dispositions of every kind, as well as to stimulate to co-operation; whereas military life exercises the faculties very partially and makes the activity of some depend on the repression of others."

One could find nowhere a more glowing and unqualified defence of peaceful activities as compared with war than in the passages which follow this in Miss Martineau's version of the *Positive Philosophy* (vol. iii, pp. 211, etc.). "By the highest and truest test that we can apply—the gradual ascendancy of the faculties of humanity over those of animality—the substitution of the industrial for the military life has raised the primitive type of social Man. The use of the understanding in practical matters is more marked in the industrial life of the moderns than in the military life of the ancients. Industrial pursuit is suitable to the intellectual mediocrity of the vast mass of the race, which can best deal with clear, concrete,

limited questions, requiring steady but easy attention, admitting of a direct or proximate solution
. . . and bringing after them a pretty certain
reward of ease and independence, in return for
sense and industry. . . . It also favours a universal
goodwill, because every man's daily toil may be
regarded as concerning others quite as much as
himself; whereas the military life encouraged the
most malignant passions in the midst of the noblest
devotedness. . . . The industrial life has unquestionably developed new intellectual and sympathetic power in the lowest class of the population
from the Middle Ages to this day. . . . It has
opened a true domestic life for the first time to
the most numerous class, there being nothing in
the condition of slaves or serfs which is worthy
of the name of family life. . . . Even free men
were not before aware of the destination of mankind at large for domestic life, being perpetually
drawn from it by the tumultuous emotions of the
city and the battlefield. . . . An industrial and
commercial life has also favoured a closer agreement between aptitude and destination" (i.e.,
appointment to posts by merit and not by birth
or caste), "and has developed that marvellous
instinctive social economy by which each industrial member is constantly employed in devising

and carrying out new methods of serving the community, every private operation assuming the character of a public function and the broad old division between the two becoming indistinguishable. . . . Much of this action arose certainly from the self-interest and cunning proper to emancipated slaves; but the love of gain is surely preferable to the love of pillage which preceded it. . . . Much of the imperfection of the industrial system is due to the absence of organization; and the rest to the imperfection of human nature; but the vices which may be remedied, and those which cannot, are a good exchange for those of a period of slavery and war."

This is only one of many passages in Comte's writings which proclaim as the supreme fact in human history the supersession of war by peaceful industry. That was the goal, and science was the means. It became the banner of a whole school of thinkers and writers, being as prominent in the teaching of St.-Simon who preceded Comte as in Herbert Spencer who followed him. In the next chapter we shall refer to events and conditions in the world which may seem to have discredited their confident judgment, but, before approaching that topic, it will be well to consider the judgment itself a little carefully. It differs in

several important points from other pacific ideals
which have appealed to the imagination of mankind in many ages, and of this ideal we are clearly
right in taking Comte as the chief author and his
presentation as the most complete. He added the
ordered and complete evolution of science to St.-
Simon's vaguer substitution of industry for war
and he used the ideal, when formed, as the basis
for the whole of religion and ethics as he conceived
them.

It will be noticed in the first place that earlier
sketches of similar hopes for the future rested not
on the gradual change and approximation of men
to one another, but on the pacifying authority of
some superior force, military or religious, impos-
ing its will on mankind. Dante and Virgil are the
most familiar examples of this idea. To Virgil the
divine Augustus, having subdued his opponents,
was then in a position to spread a Roman peace
over the whole world. But the whole world was
not known to the pacifying Roman nor did he
pause to consider how the divine ruler was to per-
petuate his own spirit even in the comparatively
small area in which for a time he had made it
prevail. The Catholic ideal which Dante presents,
extends over a larger area and finds a deeper root
in the religious consciousness of those who

accepted it. The peace of mankind lay in the will of the Supreme Ruler of all mankind. But it was a peace which grew up in the heart and conscience of believers amid fierce and internecine conflicts between rival chiefs and towns and nations in which Dante himself took a passionate part. If in one part of his nature he aspired profoundly for a radiant and heavenly peace, in another he was as keen and determined on the punishment of his enemies as any unsanctified fighter. The face might be turned towards heaven but the hands were fully armed. Now what distinguishes Comte's ideal from these and all others before his time, is that he finds it in the actual state of the world as produced by a constant process which we may trace in history. We are not asked to say that fighting was quite extinct in the world; that would have been absurd enough from a man who had lived through the many wars, aggressive and other, of two Napoleons. But we are asked to observe, and to agree, that a vast change had taken place within times quite well known to history, and that, in the time in which he was living, the general habits and occupations of the enormous majority of men, which had been transformed since fighting was the habitual occupation, went on unchanged. We shall have occasion in the next chapter to see how certain leaders of thought and rulers in post-Comtian times have been endeavouring to reverse this process. The fact makes it the more opportune to lay stress on the Comtian view, and to remember that it was generally accepted by Western thinkers, and the bulk of Western workers, for the best part of the century in which it was proclaimed.

The highest merit of Comte's view—connected with the fact that it is historical and therefore relative—lies in his appreciation both of force and of fighting, in times and places to which they were suitable, and judged by their results in building up a stronger, more united and progressive community of men. He would have agreed with Kant in finding in human nature two opposed but closely interwoven strains, the one assertive and aggressive, the other seeking companionship and response. But whereas Kant seems to have regarded these as permanent elements in perpetual conflict, Comte traces a gradual turning of the combative strain in man into efforts towards subjugating nature. We need not then postulate eternal hostility of man against man, because we see in history the steady conversion of hostile into friendly elements. Nor is there any permanent call for aggressiveness against other men as a spur

132

to action, when we have the whole universe to exercise our wits and vigour on, and men to vanquish in other competitions than those which aim at annihilating life.

The transformation is connected causally by Comte with the growth of science, but, as was pointed out above, the connexion is often indirect and many other factors have entered in. The exploration of the earth's surface and the occupation of vast new areas by agricultural and active people have been the most potent obvious factors in the industrialization of the world. Thus, in spite of the American wars with Great Britain, Mexico and Spain and their long-drawn duel over slavery among themselves, historically or sociologically one is bound to regard the settling of the United States as a colossal step towards the ideal of peace which Comte proclaimed for the world and discovered actually in being. The American Civil War came after his death; but one can hardly doubt how his sympathies would have lain, in spite of his predilection for small independent states. It was, he would have said, an inevitable though terrible price paid for the expiation of the greatest crime ever committed by Western men against the black race in the slave-trade. War is not in itself a crime, for all morality and law are relative. But universal peace makes its way, by the industrialization of the world, by the elevation of all men gradually from positions of subservience to that of freedom and self-determination and by the spread of collective thinking, which by its very nature unites mankind. The exploitation of nature, to which it also brings constantly fresh and larger bodies of workers together, organized under technical and scientific chiefs. The engineer, in this ideal of a peaceful world, takes the place of the military leader. But we have not to seek him: he is already there. What was needed in Comte's view was the realization of what had already taken place, and the conscious provision of means to secure the full good implicit in changes which had occurred only half-noticed.

"Much of the imperfection of the industrial system is due to the want of organization." In this respect one might fairly claim that the world has advanced towards the Comtian ideal, since Comte's time, on his own lines.

Organization and planning are so much the order of the day in all modern States; that one might almost say the amount of "planning" is the test of the degree of civilization in that place. Does that mean that Comte's sociology leads in practice to socialism? By no means, unless we interpret "socialism" in such a sense as to include all forms of collective and deliberate concern for the welfare of all members of a community. In that sense clearly Comte was a socialist, but he was stoutly anti-socialist in his defence of private property. That the State should own all the means of production, or that all citizens should be directly employed and salaried by the State, was far from his ideal. He looked rather to an enlargement of the powers of individual capitalists and the idea which pleased him most was "the moralization of capital," strange as it has seemed to certain minds.

It is not our purpose here, and would be far beyond the scope of this book, to sketch the contents of the four stout tomes which form the *Positive Polity*, the second of Comte's great works. He was not a man of affairs, and the various suggestions it contains, are of interest mainly as illustrating some leading principle in his thought. The moral aspect was, as we saw, supreme in all his teaching, and when, as now, we are considering the need of "organization" for the peace of the world, and the welfare and effectiveness of its workers, he would have prized most highly that type of organization which springs from the conscience and activities of free men,

135

acting voluntarily together for the general good.
The reason is obvious. Such action involves more
conviction and more effort on the part of those
who take it; and these are elements of the highest
moral value. That certain things must be sometimes enforced, either by a dictatorial majority or
a personal dictator, he would have gladly admitted.
But far above this in importance was the gradual
change of heart and habit, finding its expression
in suitable organizations, to help the weaker and
do the thing desired by free co-operation.

Were Comte therefore now completing his
survey of modern history, as leading to an ideal of
peace, he would have to add to the favourable
features, which were enumerated above, a vast
extension of organization, both voluntary and
governmental, to carry out precisely the objects
which he saw being attained, and attainable, in
such a State. So far at least we must admit the
rightness of his prescience. Want of organization
was, next to the imperfection of human nature,
the chief defect in the modern industrial system.
In the century since that thought was expressed,
the Western world has witnessed an outburst of
organization never experienced or dreamt of
before. From the League of Nations down to
the village institute, society, political, industrial,

religious and social is enmeshed in a web of organizations which leave no good object uncared for and few individuals undisturbed.

Does then the ideal of peace seem to be nearer to us, living in this state, or to Comte who forecast it? The next chapter must attempt some sort of answer.

CHAPTER IX

THE ACTUAL AND THE IDEAL

TO one who passes from the ideal of peace as
Comte pictured it, to the actual which we
have now to consider, a grave question arises on
the threshold of his inquiry. We know that
Comte's picture of the future in which he fervently
believed, included an elaborate reorganization,
especially of religion, education and social life.
There was to be a new Spiritual Power, with
priests completely trained in science and having
control both of education and public health. The
banks were to be the chief authority in the temporal
sphere and the Western Republic, of France,
England, Italy, Germany and Spain was to be the
standard-bearer of civilization for the planet. It
is not within our scope or purpose to go into
details about all this, but it is certain that Comte
proposed it and confidently expected its fulfilment
within a comparatively short time. More than a
century has now elapsed and these things have
certainly not come to pass. The movement of

events has often been diverse and in some points directly contrary. What then are we to think of his judgment as a whole? If he was provably wrong about matters in which he took the keenest interest, what guarantee have we that his reading of history is correct? Must not the foundations be rotten, if the superstructure will not stand?

The answer must take various lines and some parts of it are indicated by the question itself. It is not necessary to enter here into the much-discussed question of the continuity of Comte's life and thought. It is enough to remember that for the last period of his life, twelve years from his acquaintance with Mme. de Vaux, he became more and more absorbed in his ideals for the future and less and less in touch with the world of events and of new discoveries and research. This concentration on his own thoughts, in the midst of an intimate and sympathizing circle, is sufficient to explain the increasingly sharp outlines of his ideal State and the increasing confidence with which he expected it. It cannot be held to invalidate the judgment passed years before on the course of history, studied for its own explanation and studied by a man in the prime of life and with an active brain in contact with the best thought of his age. All that we may fairly say on the personal side, in qualification of his judgment, is that he was clearly and always of an ardent and optimistic temper. How far, and what type of, optimism is called for in the judgment of events and the conduct of life is another and larger question about which something may be said in a later chapter.

But the question we are discussing is a larger one. Apart from his special prescriptions for the future, Comte took, as we saw in the last chapter, what may well seem a favourable view of the state and prospects of the world in his time. Industry had brought general peace and there was good hope that the process would continue and proved defects be made good. The sociologist of a hundred years later, following Comte's line of thought, must note with special interest two things; one, how far the progress Comte noted has been maintained; second, how, let us say, would Comte himself have summed up the progress of mankind, were he writing in 1936 instead of in 1830–1840?

The time passed since Comte's survey is of course short enough in the span of history,—even in the small span which we describe as the history of civilization. It would be strange indeed if events had happened in that short time of sufficient weight to alter seriously, still less reverse, a judgment deliberately passed a hundred years ago on all the millennia of previous history. Yet we find undoubtedly quite a different judgment current at the present day, and a different temper in facing the future. One leading writer tells us that "humanitarianism is under a cloud," and another speaks of the "exploded superstition of the inevitability of progress." Such statements are mild specimens of a rich, new harvest of cynical questionings and timorous expectations on a field once full of certainty and hope. Is there not a *prima facie* case for explaining the facts rather as a temporary psychological phenomenon than as a serious reversal of judgments, passed not only by Comte, but by the dominant majority of sociological thinkers for the best part of a century?

Those who pass these later unfavourable judgments are not as a rule students of history, or, if they are, not of history on a wide scale. They are quite naturally moved chiefly by recent events, since the time of Comte and the other writers who made these glowing forecasts.

There are two main aspects of these events to be distinguished, corresponding, it will be noted, to the two main aspects of "humanitarianism"

which we are credibly informed is under a cloud.
On the one side, "humanity" implies a certain
attitude towards the individual man. We sympa-
thize with him and recognize certain rights of
which, as a man, he should not be deprived. Every
human being, we now feel,—though the feeling
itself is of comparatively recent date—should be
so far cared for by his fellows as to have a fair
chance of enjoying the life which he has come
into the world to share. He is alive, and so far
one of us. We cannot be indifferent to the sort
of life which falls to his lot. The other main
aspect of "humanitarianism" occupies to-day a
larger share in public controversies than the
former, larger than it did in the day of Comte; it is
by nature more controversial. It concerns the
way in which the nations and various sections
of mankind carry on their co-operation. They are,
as everyone knows, now inextricably and permanently interlocked by the links of trade and
mechanized science. They must act together
somehow; is the action easy, friendly and progressively more productive of common good?

We shall find that it is on the second aspect of
humanitarianism that the cloud has chiefly fallen
in the post-Comtian century, though even here
there is much that may be discerned, if we look

for it, as a silver lining to the cloud. It will be better, therefore, to take this second aspect first and to conclude with the former.

Two great armed conflicts have taken place since Comte's day at the very heart of Western civilization, of which the second developed in such a way as to involve nearly the whole world. The first was the Franco-Prussian War of 1870–71; the second, the Great War of 1914–18. They were intimately connected one with the other and the second is manifestly the special cause of the cloud which we are discussing.

There have also been simultaneously two general movements which have both tended to disturb the ideal of world-peace and were certainly not foreseen by Comte, at least as acting in the acute way which has been witnessed. In the first place the new nationalities which have arisen in the period have been struggling hard to secure as much trade and self-sufficient autonomy for themselves as possible; and, parallel with this the non-Western communities have been stirred to attain similar status, education and economic development as the Western states. Comte treated the latter too complacently as the undisputed leaders and guardians of the world.

From all these causes grave hindrances have arisen to the realization of the peace ideal and it is with no

143

sense of minimizing them that one asks the question, Do they essentially alter the interpretation of history which was put forward a century ago by the apostle of that ideal?

It is clear that without the bitter and unresolved difference between France and Germany, which dated from the war of 1870, the World War would not have taken place. The rival coalitions were built up round that difference and the war was chiefly fought and ultimately decided on disputed territory between those two antagonists. It follows, therefore, that when we sort out and try to understand the issues, giving to each its relative weight in the result, we shall conclude that, had the unification and settlement of Germany been peaceably accomplished when actively mooted just after Comte's death, the two catastrophes would not have happened. Such a settlement was clearly called for, in the case of one of the five essential members of the "Western Republic." It was actually prevented by the disastrous conjunction of two personalities, Bismarck and the third Napoleon. But the disastrous accident cannot be held to invalidate a general theory of peaceful progress, acting through the co-operation of nationalities. Comte himself had lived through another world-wide disturbance under the first Napoleon which went deeper in principle than the Great War, though the area affected and the resultant losses were less. The question was asked above whether the same observer, judging after the century, with the Great War and all its other disturbances included, would make the same judgment as he did in 1840. When we consider that he had made it on the morrow of the first Napoleon, the answer cannot be in doubt.

But, apart from the two wars, there are many other international facts intervening which certainly do not all weigh on the negative side. It has been noticed already that a Western Republic of five leading nations, with others clustering round according to their natural affinities, was a central part of the Comtian ideal. Of the five nations mentioned, four are at the moment members of the League of Nations and the fifth was also at one time included. The League also contains more than three-quarters of the nations of the world and the number of stably organized and independent nations is more than doubled since Comte surveyed the scene. The balance surely, if one dwells rather on things accomplished and habits set up than on dangers anticipated and losses endured, will incline even to a more favourable estimate than was possible in 1840.

There is much to be noted on the adverse side, and, as the estimate aimed at is strictly scientific and judicial, no effort should be made to minimize it. The facts which meet us, are at first sight singularly paradoxical. In a world, where the mass of the population are intent on peace as they never were before, we observe a spread of military conscription quite unknown a hundred years ago. The first Napoleon had conscripted armies, but a law of conscription was not generally in force till after the Franco-Prussian War of 1870. The conclusion seems obvious. There is not, and was never, a general recrudescence of a desire for the military life, but, in view of the dangerous and long-unhealed breach between the two neighbouring Rhineland states, a condition of unrest had been set up which prepared men's minds for a sacrifice which they always regretted, but were willing to accept for the sake of what they regarded as the safeguarding of their country. The example unfortunately spread, with the sequel of the war of 1914. The new nations, still unprotected by a strong general authority, took similar measures for their own imagined security. But it would be a mistake to regard the acceptance of compulsory service as evidence of an equally widespread acceptance of the military ideal. On the contrary, it is well known that in many cases, as for example in Switzerland, a certain measure of compulsory service is compatible with the most intensely pacific dispositions. The compulsion is not in itself dangerous, but becomes so when accompanied, as it has been lately, by violent and ill-founded excitements to the war-like spirit, uttered, as they often are, and were in the case of Napoleon, by Heads of State with their own selfish and anti-humanitarian ends in view. At the present moment, however, such incitements arouse in the minds of the great majority of mankind a feeling of repulsion and horror stronger than has ever been felt before in the history of civilized men. Therein in fact lie both the most convincing proof of a change of mind in favour of peace, and the only permanent bulwark for securing it. "*Delirant reges, plectuntur Achivi,*" is an observation of old-world wisdom. When, as now, the rulers are patently and consciously dependent on the will of the governed and have in few cases any traditional sanctity or divine right to support them, if their people truly wish for peace, they will obtain it. In this world picture, which is being compared with that of 1840, two large factors have attained an importance not allowed for by Comte. These are the British Commonwealth of Nations

147

and the United States of America, both far
weightier in the world to-day than they were
then, and both immovably attached to an ideal
of peace. Britain moved most unwillingly in the
war of 1914, and the United States much more
slowly and reluctantly. The issue was unquestionably settled by their intervention, and, more than
any other nations, these two are set against a
repetition of the experience.

Another large field of events offers ground for
tempering the optimism of Comte, but not
abandoning his ideal or denying the substantial
truth of his general judgment. He was, as we
have seen, absorbed beyond measure in the spread
of sound ideas and the triumph of reason in the
world. As Western people had manifestly developed
the structure of modern science, which is the most
powerful factor in moulding events, it was, in his
view, to be expected that Western thought would
lead the less scientifically prepared people with
their glad consent. In one sense this has proved
to be the case, for everywhere Western ideas and
inventions have obtained a vogue which tends to
make the world a unified place in a less lovely or
interesting way than idealists might desire.
Common mathematics and science are less obvious
to the eye than common film-pictures and motor-

cars. And in other and more aggressive forms the Westernization of the world has brought anxiety on the West which initiated it. The keen-witted Japanese are but one of the old peoples, feverishly modernized, who, by adopting Western methods, have increased the commercial and political competition of the nations and made the easy primacy of Comte's Western Republic more uncertain. Such questions, as how the factory products of a quick and efficient people, using scientific methods but living on a far simpler standard, are to be assimilated by mankind, without a general lowering of the standard, are not to be solved, merely by abstract religious canons of living for the race. How to live, and even life itself, become insistent problems for tens of millions who have no animosity against the workers of any other race, but ask for such an application of science and the common mind as will enable all to live in amity on an earth rich enough to feed all her children. The problem in short, like so many more, has proved in practice to be infinitely more complex and difficult than it appeared to the optimists of the first generation of humanitarians.

As a centre of such collective thinking and planning, the League of Nations is clearly the largest new definite factor in the world, the heaviest item on the credit side in the fresh survey. It is neither a Spiritual Power, such as Comte envisaged, nor the World State of our contemporary, more politically minded, Utopians. But it has in it elements akin to both conceptions. Less idealist or logical than Comte or his countrymen would have framed it, it appeared to the English and American minds, chiefly responsible for its creation, to be the best practical expedient for meeting the emergency of the moment. It was thus framed rather on British practical lines of compromise and the possibility of growth and adjustment. Neither purely consultative, nor efficiently executive (as the government of a World State), it has had to feel its way. It has disappointed many hopes, but avoided many disasters. On a balanced view it must be held to have kept the world far more peaceful than it would otherwise have been and on the whole to have gained in strength. When one has, as at present (in the spring of 1936), over fifty nations co-operating in an attempt to redress a breach of treaty obligations and suppress a war, one cannot regard the new situation as a retrogression. The very efforts so made, though slower and less effective than every believer in an international world would desire, are a new phenomenon, and those who belittle them, do not realize the profound general changes of mind on which they rest. If again one applies the sort of canons of judgment which a sociological view of history would dictate, one must hold that new facts in consonance with a general movement are more likely to survive and make new growth than those contrary to that movement. Does any one question that the world is far more actually interlocked, by thought and the applications of science, now than it ever was? If it is, those institutions, acts and events which are in consonance with that tendency may be reasonably expected to persist and to prevail. That is the type of prediction which sociology permits and encourages. No one can predict exactly how the present war in Abyssinia will end: everyone may safely conclude from history that organs for expressing collective thought and carrying out collective decisions, of which the League of Nations, though the greatest, is only one, must establish themselves and grow in strength. Comte's dictum indeed is as true now as a hundred years ago, that, next to imperfections in human nature, a want of organization is the greatest defect in collective affairs. In his days the remark was most obviously to be applied to internal industry which had led millions to a

151

state of ignoble and monotonous poverty, in spite of large capitalist gains. Since his time, that type of evil has been largely remedied and a pathway has been blazed in all industrialized countries for further advance. We may repeat the dictum now with more special reference to international affairs, but when we do so, it should be remembered that the framework of the needed organization has been created, and that the creation itself was not anticipated by practical men a hundred years ago.

But there is one whole department of human effort—in the view of many thinkers the most important of all—in which organization and successful effort have been applied, since Comte's time, with results beyond his dreams or those of any other man of science of that time. This is the region of Social Medicine, organized and administered usually by what would have been called in those days "socialist" States.

The story of this advance is little known, and there is no comprehensive work in English to which reference could be made. Happily, a countryman of Comte's, M. René Sand, has recently taken the trouble to put all the facts together in a rational form and his survey[1] gives

[1] *L'Economie Humaine par le Médicine Sociale*. Rieder, Paris. Now translated : *Health and Human Progress*. Kegan Paul.

us the most substantial evidence of human better-
ment in the century, which we possess. It is
most right and relevant to include it as a
development of Comte's ideal, for in his view the
work of physicians was religious, equal in value,
if not superior, to that of any other servants of
mankind. In the century since he wrote they have
worked with more palpable and measurable
advantage to mankind than any other class of
workers. It is difficult to know which of the
overwhelming multitude of facts to select to make
the amelioration most apparent. . . . Life, it is
assumed, is a valuable thing. The efforts of organized medicine aim at increasing its amount and
enabling the larger number who live, to enjoy
living with less mutilation, infirmity and anxiety
for their latter end.

The increase effected in the amount of life pre-
served is perhaps the most striking of all the figures.
Two hundred years ago only a minority of the
infants born survived, sometimes quite a small
minority. In the seventeenth and eighteenth
centuries in England at least fifty persons in every
thousand died per annum. In Comte's time, in
the first two-thirds of the nineteenth century, in
all countries the number was over thirty. Now no
country which furnishes returns—and there are

some fifty of them,—reaches that figure, and in
the large majority the number is under twenty.
In Great Britain it is twelve; in Australia and
New Zealand under nine. The expectation of life
therefore has grown steadily in all countries since
exact returns were kept, i.e., since science was
admitted as a handmaid to government. In a
hundred years in England, it has increased from
forty to over fifty years, and similarly in all cases,
exactly in proportion to the degree in which the
nation has cultivated its medical knowledge and
organized its application.

The banishment of the old plagues, thought
inevitable, has become a commonplace. Leprosy,
cholera, typhus and many more fell diseases, now
no longer ravage—except in the rarest cases—
Western Europe. We are concentrating rightly
on those that remain, cancer and even the common
cold. But it is unscientific to ignore what has
been accomplished, especially for the sociologist
whose sheet anchor is a law of progress.

It is strange that humanitarianism should be
thought to be under a cloud at the time when the
facts suggest a stronger daylight than we have
yet enjoyed. Unless, which is doubtless the
explanation of the paradox, we grow less aware
of things, less inclined to treat them as a boon and

a gospel, the more familiar they become. Who talks about the fine weather at the Cape or in the Pacific, where one may revel in the sunshine all day long?

We have been passing almost imperceptibly to that larger and vaguer aspect of humanitarianism which was mentioned above, and is really fundamental to the more special aspect which is expressed in various forms of international relations. The large aspect is the moral or religious feeling of the worth and dignity of every individual merely as a man, whatever his race or condition. Socialized medicine is, of course, mainly inspired by this frame of mind in the societies which are practising it, while the League of Nations and other international organizations lend it valuable aid. Comte, had he been making this revised survey, would have laid most stress on the moral advance which it implies, and it is well to note that point here, because it is essential to Comte's sociology of history. He held most emphatically that man does advance morally as well as intellectually; it is in fact impossible to divorce the two aspects of his nature. And the gain made, is—taking the wide view of the race as a whole—a permanent acquisition. Now in Comte's view of morality the supreme thing is making the social prevail over the selfish. He would have accepted as a definition of virtuous action the effort over one's self in the interests of others, and the connexion of this view with the growth of a humanitarian spirit is obvious. Judged by that test, the moral advance of mankind in the last century is beyond dispute; the most considerable, it might seem—if we take the numbers affected into account—in the history of the race.

It has sometimes been objected that the humanitarian work which is so marked a feature of recent history, is rather a collective effort of democratic societies, inspired by their own selfish interests, than the spontaneous action of men concerned for the welfare of their fellows, and that the individual remains as selfish, perhaps more selfish than before. No doubt it is true that many works of charity, once performed by individuals, are now, in our modern socialized states, done by governmental action, and that there is constant pressure that more should be done. No doubt also, especially in Christian days, there have always been many good and kindly persons ready to pity and relieve the sufferings of others. But it is equally clear that, in the recent period in which humanitarianism became a gospel, a new sentiment has become diffused, which adds to pity another feeling that, the man, whoever he may be, has claims and possibilities which society should promote, in its own interests as well as his. The pity and sympathy, if not more intense than they have ever been, are certainly now far more generalized, and a sense of human worth has come in to crown them. It is a demonstrable sequel to the triumphs of man achieved since the birth of modern science and was anticipated by the greatest exponents of science in the seventeenth and eighteenth centuries.

The consciousness that we all have of these things, is their best proof, though there is abundance of evidence in detail. The treatment of children, servants and all subordinate or afflicted persons has been revolutionized in little over a hundred years. In classical antiquity, from which our civilization has descended, the exposure of unwanted children in baskets in lonely places was regularly practised. Christianity had made that impossible, but had not prevented the death of the majority born, until within two hundred years of to-day. In the thirties of the last century a child of thirteen was hanged at Maidstone and another of nine condemned to death, though not executed, for a trifling theft from a shop. On a larger scale, to the greed of employers and parents in the factories, thousands of children of even younger age were regularly sacrificed. Down to the nineteenth century men and women crowded to executions and to whippings and tortures as a pleasurably exciting spectacle. Many of these exhibitions now appear to us so revolting and inexpressible that one would hardly be excused for putting the details on paper. But they may be read in quite authentic records,—the deliberate stirring up of madmen behind iron bars, the giving of negroes as food to dogs, and multitudes of similar horrors. It is hard sometimes to combine that warm affection and respect for one's ancestors which should be a part of true religion, with an accurate knowledge of the filth and brutalities which they constantly tolerated and often enjoyed.

That these things have now become inconceivable to us is not merely owing to the force of a law imposed by a superior few on an unregenerate majority. The mass themselves have changed, though law contributes to sustain the change. It is the mass which would now be revolted by the performance of brutal things once treated as a matter of course, and the gain is general. It may be expected to be as permanent as the passing of slavery and the gladiatorial games.

The changes of this kind which have marked the last century are specially relevant to Comte's sociology because he made the evolution of humanity in all its senses the leading thread in history. If men gained a heightened sense of one-ness with their fellows, the rest would follow; assuming only that their intellectual faculties were not weakened, of which the progress of science gives no hint. The heart should inspire action and the intellect only guides the steps to the ideal of universal love which a good heart proclaims. This view of morality, as the growth of the social spirit and the subordination of the individual to the whole, is at the centre of all Comte's system; it gave Humanity as the last term of the social series, and, if we are to judge the last century as he would have judged it, we must make that consideration paramount. It cannot, we think, be denied that, if we do so, the verdict, with many heavy deductions, will be on the favourable side. He would have regarded the Great War as a terrible calamity, avoidable by a better use of human foresight and hurried on by the wicked perversity of a few blind men. But, as the wars of the Revolution and of Napoleon were surmounted and should be regarded as the price of human emancipation at that time, so, to the farseeing mind, the Great War would appear as the price of world-wide nationalities and their inevitable peaceful co-operation. But, beyond the tentative and halting efforts that are being made on the international plane, he would have marked as signal triumphs of the social spirit the development of national organizations for public welfare all over the civilized world. Nothing comparable to this in magnitude or efficiency has ever been attempted before, and is by no means in itself antagonistic to the wider ideal of international union. In rightly lamenting the deficiencies of the latter, we are too often apt to overlook what has been successfully, sometime marvellously, accomplished in the former field. It is in various degrees common to all.

One case in Great Britain is illustrative of many and the student of social progress may fairly use it, for, with due allowance for difference of circumstance, the comparative method is applicable in the sciences of life, including mankind. After the Napoleonic wars, with no organized social services, a far smaller number of discharged soldiers returned to civil life; and the country had been far less disturbed, socially and economically,—though those wars were longer,—than it was during the Great War. Yet, judged by every test, the period immediately succeeding Waterloo was one of the most disturbed and distressed in English annals. Violent and destitute men went marching about the country. It was the time of Peterloo and the Six Acts, of "Queen Mab" and the "Mask of Anarchy." A hundred years later, after the greatest war in history, in which England had lost over two million lives and had to put every available man in the field and strain every domestic nerve to avert starvation, five million men, trained to arms, were restored in two years to civil employment, without the firing of a shot or a whisper of civil disorder. Does not the reality of social and moral progress shine indisputably from such amazing facts? They speak without mystery, for the facts are evident. In the decade before the War our present system of social services had been inaugurated and provision made for all aged people, with insurance against unemployment. The problem of disbandment was carefully studied beforehand and provision made for its proper distribution in time and the temporary assistance of the men disbanded. The special problem was isolated and worked out in detail in an atmosphere of higher social responsibility and infinitely more competent governmental technique. What would have seemed impossible a hundred years before was accomplished without difficulty. Is there no moral for the problems of international relations?

CHAPTER X

THE ACTUAL IN SOCIOLOGY

IT is no fanciful illusion to see an analogy between
the relative advances made in the practical
spheres of humanitarian action and those in the
spheres of abstract thinking. It is indeed of the
very essence of Comte's teaching to trace the
connexion between them. Right thinking, he
held, must precede right doing. Now, in the
last chapter, we traced an unmistakable increase
in humanitarian feeling in that period. Savage
laws had been amended and a more humane and
merciful attitude was diffused, with a greater
respect for the individual claims of human beings
as men and women. We also noticed—perhaps
the most noticeable of all the changes—an extraordinary development of social technique, by
which in the range of national action results have
been achieved which would have been quite
inconceivable a hundred years ago. The demobiliza-
tion of 1919 was a conspicuous example. So is
the organization of elementary education in this

country, and the postal services here and elsewhere. Broadcasting is now providing another signal triumph. It is not surprising that on the international, world-wide plane the success achieved is less complete. Three things militate against it. The circumstances become far more complex, being a multiplication of the difficulties of the separate nations co-operating, by the number of the nations. Then obstacles of temper, prejudice and sectional interest are added. The separate nation sometimes irrationally prefers its own separation. Lastly, the driving-force of a collective passion becomes weaker as we extend its area to the limit. The nation has a strong belief in the excellence and worthiness of its own arrangements and its own ends. But some people —M. Bergson for instance—assert that the excellence and worthiness of an ideal of Humanity, embracing everyone, is so remote and complicated as to be quite unattainable in practice.

Now this difficulty in practice, which constantly faces the orator at Geneva, is also—perhaps even more seriously—an obstacle in theory. In every branch of knowledge separate areas, like nations, have been staked out in the last hundred years, and each, by reason of the simultaneous and colossal growth of the number of facts to be

163

correlated, has become more than enough for the life-work of the most industrious man. Thus the old ideal of a comprehensive science, such as Comte pictured his sociology to be, has become more and more remote. One of the latest, best equipped and sympathetic writers[1] on the subject ends a recent book with these words: "The conception of a self-directing humanity is new and as yet vague in the extreme. To work out its full theoretical implications, and, with the aid of other sciences, to inquire into the possibilities of its realization, may be said to be the ultimate object of sociology." Comte in fact began at the end of sociology. Appearing sometimes to himself, and often to his closer followers, as the Joshua of the promised land, he was actually the Moses, gifted with a vision of the distant goal but never entering in. Of the general inspiration which he has bequeathed to later workers we shall speak in the next chapter. Of the work which has followed him under the special title of "sociology," one can only speak here in the most fragmentary and tentative way.

If we were to judge of the importance of any man merely by the volume of the work following him under the title which he used, there could

[1] Prof. Morris Ginsberg: *Sociology.* Home University Library.

be no doubt that Comte would, with Darwin, rank first among the thinkers of the nineteenth century. *Sociology* and *Positive* in the one case; *Evolution* and *Natural Selection* in the other, having about equal celebrity. A number of the American journal *Social Studies* (July 1935) is sufficient proof. It contains two closely printed articles of some forty pages giving an account of "The Literature of Sociology" for the one year of 1934, and the writers apologize for attempting to crowd so much into so small a space. To appreciate the magnitude of the spate, it should be remembered that this list is mainly of English and, still more of American, works and that they all appeared within one year of the century which has elapsed since the foundation of sociology. The writers comment upon the catalogue in words which throw much light on the question to be discussed in this and the next chapter. How far has the founder of sociology been followed and justified by his successors? They point out that towards the end of the nineteenth century a great change came over the general aim and spirit of sociological research. Up to that time the "all-absorbing interest was system-building, resulting in grandiose productions such as those of Auguste Comte, Herbert Spencer and Lester Ward." But with the

organization of the American Sociological Society
in 1905 a change came over the scene. A new
and more strictly scientific age seemed to be opening for sociology, and since then sociologists
have been much more concerned with concrete
analysis of social processes than with the nature
of society, with empirical social research rather
than with speculative social philosophy. What
has been lost in breadth has in some respects been
compensated for by a wealth of detail. Sociological literature has become less inclusive but
more precise.

So far the judgment seems rather favourable
to what has taken place, but the authors are quite
alive to another side of the question. While the
natural sciences have each achieved a common
universe of discourse, with a frame of reference
in which the concepts have a fairly precise and
stable meaning, in sociology the case is very
different. Specialization here has proceeded without corresponding integration or organization,
until the present state of things approaches the
chaotic. There is not only a noticeable lack of
agreement on fundamental concepts and assumptions, but no clearly recognized division of labour
or of funding knowledge in order to secure continuity and order.

The picture drawn is especially true of the United States, where work and literature nominally "sociological," is far more abundant than anywhere else, but the description of the state of the science is true generally. Nothing human seems at first sight less like the sociology of Comte than the scheme of study propounded by these authors, who are in touch with sociologists all over the world, and their scheme is much like that of most other sociologists except that it goes into more detail. It would take too much space to give either this or any other scheme. Originally sociology was to consist of two main branches, the static and the dynamic, and to be based on a connected study of the lower sciences culminating in biology. But one finds that nearly the whole, at least of the American scheme would be contained in what Comte called the static aspect of the subject, i.e., the study of how people actually live together, while the dynamic aspect of development hardly finds a place at all. In the American scheme "history" only appears as the History of Sociology. In Comte's scheme, as we saw, the history of the advance-guard of the human race forms the bulk of the volume of his *Positive Philosophy* devoted to sociology.

It rests with writers of "Introductions to

Sociology" to offer their solutions of the apparently inextricable tangle. Only three things can be attempted here; First, to inquire briefly what has happened in the science and why; Second, to consider how the Comtian principles would apply to the conditions which have arisen; Third, to name—it can hardly be more than a name—a few of the writers in the sociological field who have done most to influence the study, consciously or unconsciously, in a Comtian sense.

The specialization and dispersion of effort so vividly and truly depicted by the American critics is a common feature in recent research, very noticeable in biology, inevitable in a study which sets out to embrace the human race, actual and historical. The phenomenon is paralleled among the successors of Darwin. They too have fallen upon his "grandiose" scheme and discussed it in infinite detail. What is a variation, and how do variations really occur, etc.? Happily for Darwin he had been all his life a most patient and minute worker, and his definite results were less liable to be called in question than the historical facts or scientific judgments of Comte. But the general attitude, and sometimes the language used, are very similar in the two cases; and in each case there was much room for the widest inquiry and strengthening the main supports of the original theory. In Comte's case it is obvious, from the nature of his upbringing, from his sensitive secluded character and the character of the times in which he lived, that his sociology on the static side would be highly coloured and incomplete. He had not the social sympathy or the knowledge of men and countries needed for a broad sure judgment of how men live now and how they are likely to act in future. Considering the limits of his personal vision, his intuition, based on second-hand knowledge and scientific inference, is often marvellous. But the wide inquiry of which the American school are the chief exemplars was and is essential. It was needful to add the spirit of a Le Play to that of a Comte to redress the balance. But it has now dipped rather heavily on the Le Play side.

For both English and American workers have done yeomen service in the school of Le Play, none better than Charles Booth and his successors in London who have given us the two complementary and monumental studies in detail of *Life and Labour* in the largest urban community in the world. Geddes, with his *Outlook Towers* and *Town Planning*, Branford with his *Regional Surveys*, are essentially workers in the same field.

169

Another strain of thought and temper has become prominent in the present century, and especially since the Great War, which works powerfully *against* the direction for which Comte stands. This is the tendency to deny the progressive triumph of reason in human affairs and to lay stress on the irrational. Those, like the Americans and the planners of Regional Surveys— what are sometimes called "field naturalists" in sociology,—are preliminary workers who accumulate the raw material for later scientific synthesis. The accumulators of the irrational do nothing directly towards this end but provide pathological cases which may illustrate the normal working of the organism when this has been established by other means. This perverted point of view, the concentration on the morbid, must be attributed largely to the mental shock of the Great War. It will take us some years yet to overcome it. The sudden upheaval of a long-established peaceful evolution, the plunge of a whole civilized and highly organized world into a gigantic effort at self-destruction, was well calculated to destroy our belief in the sanity of mankind. It might, as we can now see, have been avoided by a variety of comparatively small re-adjustments; and yet, in that ever-memorable case, the irrational prevailed. Little wonder that so many minds, not strengthened by the long view of man's age-long uprising from the slime and his inherent stability, lost faith for a time. There could be no more confidence in reason and the common good. Of this temper, which is amply illustrated in all contemporary literature, Pareto is the best example in sociology. He attracts his readers largely because he appeals to the same spirit in them. His uncouth and unilluminating phraseology are forgiven for the zest and piquancy with which he unrolls his voluminous record of human crime and folly. The eminent reviewer,[1] enlisted to recommend his work, makes no scruple of laying stress on this aspect of it. "It was not solely an ardent passion for scientific truth that sustained him through his gigantic labours, it was also, I suspect, for the pleasure of sardonically laughing that he worked his way through libraries and files of contemporary newspapers in search of the documents with which his theories are so copiously illustrated. Endlessly appalled and endlessly amused by the bottomless stupidity of his fellowmen, Flaubert spent seven years collecting the materials for his great and, alas, unfinished epic of human imbecility, *Bouvard et Pécuchet*. Pareto

[1] Mr. Aldous Huxley.

171

I believe, was moved by the same strange passion and his Treatise is (among other things) a museum of stupidities vaster even than Flaubert's chamber of horrors. Pareto moves among the monstrous exhibits making an occasional dry comment that reveals the intensity of his excruciating delight in the spectacle. . . . He conceived it to be his duty as a man of science to make no ethical comments, formulate no ideals." Here clearly we reach, not the negative want, but the positive opposite of Comte's ideal.

Another strain of recent and contemporary thought has contributed widely and deeply in the same direction. This is the tendency in psychology to lay increasing stress on the subconscious. It has been noticed in earlier chapters that to Comte the word "psychology" bore, like "metaphysics," mostly an unfavourable connotation. He was prejudiced against its use by what he considered the aberrations of the leading psychological schools of his day, especially of Victor Cousin and Jouffroy, who set out to derive an interpretation both of the self and of the world from introspection, from an analysis of the Ego. Not wishing that his philosophy of the mind should be confounded with theirs, he discarded the word altogether as representing an independent science in his system and preferred to speak of its subject-matter under the two aspects under which he held that it might be rightly studied. On the one hand, it belonged to physiology, so far as we were studying its biological organs, either in ourselves or other animals. On the other hand, so far as mental products were concerned, it was a part of sociology. In this analysis subsequent thinkers would in the main agree, though they would add that introspection, properly corrected and controlled, cannot be discarded, as it affords our only approach to any knowledge at all.

Social Psychology now takes its place rightly as one of the subdivisions of contemporary sociology. But into this field a strongly disturbing element has in the present century been introduced by the cult of the sub-conscious as representing the fundamental and most powerful forces in the determination of all action. The Freudian technique is now so familiar that we need not dwell on its detail, but it is important to note the way in which it diverts attention from the growth of the newer and more ideal aspects of the mind and thus infects sociology with a spirit directly contrary to the direction of Comte, allies it, in fact, with that belief in the force of the irrational which was noticed above.

173

Now neither Comte, nor any other philosopher, questions the reality of a subconscious basis in the mind. It had been noticed and studied, less minutely, by numerous thinkers before an age which loves to trace everything to a psychological source. Let it do so; neither Comte nor his sympathizers will disagree, if the mind for which we look, is a social and forward-looking mind, not one which finds its inspiration in a low origin, but in a high destiny. The psychology most deserving of study is that which shows how from its low sources, common with the brutes, a high directing force has arisen in which all minds co-operate but the highest tend always to take the lead. To study this force is to strengthen it, and every form of analysis which disintegrates the ideal and proclaims it only to consist of the baser elements which it contains, degrades and weakens it. It is no more the scientific truth to say that filial affection derives from a sexual impulse than it would be to say that the soldier dies on the battlefield from blood-lust or that the statesman serves his country for a title or that Michel Angelo painted the Sistine Chapel for the pay of Julius II. The supreme task of the social psychologists who in this sense should form the headquarters staff of sociology, is to show how in the various

subdivisions of human life and thought the mind
has gained control. It gains control because it is
social, and it gains more and more settled control
in so far as it looks to the future. These are the
highest truths of social psychology. They may
be traced in Comte, but they have been obscured
by recent tendencies in psychology. It remains to
see where, in post-Comtian thought, most has
been done to carry on work of this kind, arising
from, or congenial to, the most fruitful truth to
be derived from him.

Surveying generally the field of Western European thought, an interesting and highly significant
fact appears. It is in France and England, the
pioneers of progress in the eighteenth and nineteenth centuries, the countries where Comte
received in his lifetime the most cordial recognition, that the synthetic aspect of sociology has
been most fully cultivated since. For it will be
seen at once that nothing less than this is at stake.
If we are to entertain any hope of bringing the
various studies which rank as sociological, together
and of giving them any collective meaning and
purpose, it must be through the study of the evolution of mind. This is the specially human factor
in which men co-operate incessantly, universally
and progressively, and nothing else, certainly not

the geographical nor the economic nor even the artistic factors can exhibit so well this progressive evolution. It is equally clear that French and English thinkers, whether they derive explicitly from Comte or not, are those in all the world who have shown themselves most conscious of this truth. To take first examples on the outskirts of Western civilization which show a difference; America we have noticed above. She has now put aside the early attempts at an intellectual synthesis which were derived from Western sources, and revels in an abundance of disconnected efforts and inquiries which might form the basis for co-ordinated results, if a desire or a scheme for co-ordination existed. Lester Ward, who was the strongest mind who ever attempted in America the rôle of synthesis, has passed away, and most of his influence with him. His work has still great interest for students of our special subject, for, being himself an accomplished man of science, and starting as a sociologist rather under the stimulus of Herbert Spencer, he found on careful inquiry that on most of the great questions which divided Spencer and Comte, he was led ultimately to side with Comte. For the rest, American sociological practice has followed Spencer, whose multifarious inquiries, without a leading idea, are typical of most of the work seen in that country since. Russia, which forms the Eastern, as the United States the Western, annex of Europe, was occupied busily, until the Bolshevik revolution, in absorbing the latest ideas of Western thinkers. They leaned in turn, first, to the most materialistic interpretation of modern science, then to an extreme idealism. With the Bolsheviks, Marx has taken control and found his kingdom. Again one is struck by the want of balance, by their whole-hearted acceptance of one highly prejudiced and unbalanced reading of human affairs. It might be said with some truth that the extreme solutions, both in practice and theory, which have found favour in Russia, have done much to push their neighbours in Germany to another extreme. Naziism is largely the counterblast to Communism, and as a serious sociological interpretation of events hardly deserves notice. But it is noticeable that Germany, before the advent of National Socialism, had already shown herself more inclined than her Western neighbours to stand apart. With great exceptions as in the age of Lessing, Herder and Goethe, the social spirit in Germany has tended to embody itself rather in the form of the Volksgeist than of Humanity. Comte never had a hearing there in his lifetime, and little since, from either philosophic or practical thinkers in Germany. Such prominent names in German sociology, as Simmel and Vierkandt for instance, stand for a sociology which would be rather another specialism than the synthesis of social studies aimed at by the school of sociologists who stand in the main stream which descends from Comte and his sympathizers.

There can be no doubt of this affiliation, if one looks fairly into the literature of the subject in France and England. In his lifetime Comte's material existence was guaranteed by his supporters in France and England. Had this not been forthcoming, the earlier work, on the positive philosophy, which had been finished while he was still teaching could hardly have found the general recognition that it did, and the later work which became more and more synthetic, could not have been attempted. He spoke and taught as a prophet, supported by a band of disciples more or less complete, nearly all of them from England and France; and while the larger band came naturally from his own country, the English included perhaps a larger proportion of weighty and representative people, and on the moral and religious side the English following was more thorough and convinced. The sequel in the succeeding century has been true to this initial direction, though we are speaking here purely of the sequel in the philosophic and scientific sense.

A stray thinker from elsewhere, such as Paul Barth, once of Leipzig, may be of Comtian lineage, but in France and Italy (much akin to France intellectually), and in England, a steady influence has remained throughout and notable work done avowedly on Comtian suggestion, besides the generally more synthetic turn which sociology has striven to maintain in the country of its origin and in England. Many have been inspired "à refaire l'œuvre de Comte," and in attempting to do it, have contributed solid additions to knowledge or applied some of his leading thoughts more thoroughly in various detailed lines. The examples given must perforce be somewhat haphazard and fragmentary, as the subject is vast and, though cognate, is not the special subject of this book.

In France, as was seen in an earlier chapter, the general significance of Comte in philosophy has been much better appreciated than elsewhere, while their prominent sociologists more clearly bear his mark. Of the more general type of thinker Alfred Fouillée is perhaps the best example, whose appreciation would approximate closely to that suggested in these pages. Of the sociologists proper Durkheim, the most eminent and the most prolific, is in the direct descent. He is Comtian in his stress on the function of sociology as a unitary discipline, though less than Comtian in dwelling far more on the social quality of the actual than in tracing the evolution of the actual from the past by any ascertainable law. He held too that one could only study sociologically the separate societies of man and that Humanity was rather a regulating idea, "un être de raison."[1]

But there is a whole class of sociological workers, whose claims as sociologists are not generally acknowledged, and who derive more directly and openly from Comte than most of those who monopolize the title. These are the historians of science, to which, as in the case of George Sarton, the addition of "civilization" is very properly made.

Mr. Sarton, though by birth a Belgian, may well be included among the French contingent of the continuers of Comte, and he claims that distinction himself, for it is to him we owe the phrase "refaire l' œuvre de Comte" which has been

[1] Durkheim : *Les Règles de la Méthode Sociologique*, 6th edn. p. 26.

privately admitted by many of those engaged in the researches of which Mr. Sarton is the most distinguished and prolific exponent. American generosity has for some years given him a home since he lost his library in Belgium during the War. But he remains one of the most perfect international humanists of our time and does a work of general enlightenment and unification in *Isis*, which has never been approached by any other student. There are, however, many other workers in the same field, Meyerson and Paul Tannery, to name only two of the most distinguished among the dead. All these men, exploring the history of thought, have given grateful recognition to the inspiration of Comte, even though in many cases they have been compelled in the course of their work to combat some special doctrine enounced by Comte. It is the fact that they in particular look back to Comte, and that their work has consisted in tracing the evolution of science, which make their inclusion here so necessary and significant. Far as we still are from the goal, it is here, in the synthesis of thought and action, that we must seek for the master-thought in sociology. Since Comte's day, broadly speaking, we are faced by an enormous and ever-growing mass, on the one hand,

of facts as to the way of life both of dead and
living men, and, on the other, of the records
of men's thoughts in the building up of theory.
But the two spheres remain for the most part
quite distinct, so much so indeed that the term
"sociologist" is not even commonly applied to
the latter class. Yet they are the men who stand
most directly in the succession of the founder.
It is a strange and bewildering sight. Already
in this book at least four great departments of
human studies have been necessarily mentioned,
which all now stand apart, and in some cases claim
loudly their independent methods and validity.
History, claiming primarily to be political;[1]
Sociology, turning mainly to field studies of how
men live; the History of Science, concerning itself
exclusively with the growth of theory; Philosophy,
owning no allegiance to or connexion with, either,
but having a history of philosophy in another
world. Was Comte entirely visionary and futile
in trying to envisage a scheme in which all these
workers might find a place together? Is there
to be no paradise in this world, where the lions
and lambs of theory may lie down together, no
doctrine of childlike sympathy to guide them?

---

[1] Thus Sir J. A. R. Marriott in the *Quarterly Review*, January,
1936: "The historian *must* be a politician."

One man, who had some hope of this, deserves special commemoration here, for he was an Englishman, the first holder of a chair of sociology in this country, and a man who stood in a close and sympathetic, but by no means servile, attitude to Comte. This was L. T. Hobhouse, who died in 1928 and was the first Martin White Professor of Sociology at the London School of Economics. His story and his work call for rather longer comment.

He was an Oxford student and passed through the discipline of ancient history and philosophy which the School of "Literæ Humaniores" provides. He taught in this school at Oxford for a time, but the quiet and traditional ways of Oxford could never have satisfied him, and he sought a busier life of more immediate contact with the problems of the day. This led him to journalism which for the greater part of his life divided his interest with philosophical writing and teaching. But before he plunged into it he had strengthened his scientific foundations by working seriously in a laboratory at Oxford on the physiology of the brain. Now it happened that he came into intimate and long-continued relations with a man who was acknowledged by all who knew him to be the ablest of the immediate English disciples of

183

Comte. This was Dr. J. H. Bridges, who served a long official life as Medical Inspector to the (then) Local Government Board, and in his leisure wrote many admirable essays, illustrating the thought of the man he never hesitated to call his Master. Now Bridges and Hobhouse had married sisters, and through these affectionate family ties Hobhouse came constantly in touch with the thought of Comte, expounded by the older man who had been a member of the original circle of sympathizers, had known George Eliot and Lewes and was a contemporary and life-long friend of Frederic Harrison. Hobhouse, having passed through Oxford after the Hegelian wave, was fully alive to all sides of the philosophical debate. Being an open-minded and generous nature, he resented the slight put upon J. S. Mill in his day at Oxford. He determined to do something to rehabilitate Mill, and was all the time absorbing general ideas derived from Comte, who was one of Mill's chief formative forces.

No environment could have been more favourable for producing a frame of mind, able to criticize Comte, able at the same time to absorb Comte's seminal ideas and do justice to him. Apart from all his work in other fields, he sketched out a complete system of sociology in the cycle of

The Rational Good, The Elements of Social Justice and *Social Development*, and he gave a metaphysical basis to the whole in his *Development and Purpose*. He is perhaps the nearest to Comte of all post-Comtian sociologists in following what we hold to be the most important truth in Comte's system, viz., that the evolution of mind is, or should be, the guiding principle in sociology. Hobhouse went straight to this point in his earliest writings, *The Theory of Knowledge, Mind in Evolution* and *Morals in Evolution*. But while conscious of the supreme importance of this side of his subject, he never neglected the more practical or static aspects, taking part with others in an inquiry into "The Material Culture and Social Institutions of Simpler Peoples," after the London Chair and the School of Sociology had come into being. He would have done more than even the wonderful record which stands to his name, had he not been hindered by two grave causes. One was the want of any existing organization for the study or teaching of sociology in England. He was a pioneer, working in an atmosphere of distracting public troubles and with little general sympathy for his scientific aims among the older educational institutions in the country. The other cause which hampered, while it stimulated him, was his passionate interest in those questions of justice, freedom and peace which were agitating the world as much in his time as in ours. He gave as much care and energy to these as to his theoretical studies. The social and political world in England is better, above all juster, for his work. But the task of co-ordinating those studies and of bringing history and philosophy in due relation to sociology, to which he put his hand in the right direction, still remains as a supreme duty both in the educational and scientific spheres.

CHAPTER XI

IT was noticed in an early chapter that, while
the primacy of Comte in sociology is generally
acknowledged by sociologists, they are often
at pains to point out that what they understand
and practise under that name, is something very
different from what the founder and namer of
the science had in mind. Most of their work,
as we saw in the last chapter, fully confirms this
statement. It becomes therefore an interesting
problem to estimate, in broad and somewhat
speculative outline, wherein his life's work and
thought have borne fruit. This is a far more
difficult question with a thinker than with a man
of action. With a statesman, a successful soldier
or an inventor, we can point with confidence to
something accomplished. Had he not lived, so
far as we can see, that particular thing, with all
its consequences, would have been different.
But with a thinker it is otherwise, and the more
philosophic he is, the less is it possible with

certainty to assign definite results to his work. It may be, and often is, far more profound and extensive in its effects than the work of the practical man, but it is always more elusive, and, if philosophic, it brings together the thought of multitudes of others who may fairly claim to be regarded as partners. As Comte was one of the most ambitious and comprehensive of thinkers, this consideration must apply in a high degree to him. Yet it does not seem impossible to disengage certain great directing ideas from the intellectual atmosphere which would not be there, or would be there in far less clearness and force, if he had not made them his own and spent his life in propagating them. It may be a useful way of summing up this volume, to try and do this and give these ideas a brief clear statement.

The first and dominating idea in all his work was that of Humanity. To trace this in earlier thought throughout the ages, would be to give the intellectual genealogy of Comte; one must be content to begin with the Romans from whom we derive the word. Cicero, of course, has it and when we turn to Cicero, it may sometimes seem that there is little in the modern usage which may not find its root in him. But the impression would be misleading, for, as with all the greatest ideas embodied in ancient words, the final value rests in the richness and variety of the contents which the word has acquired from the millions of minds which have used, enlarged and handed it down. Put, therefore, beside any Ciceronian usage of the word "humanitas," such a passage as the following from a junior contemporary of Auguste Comte, Sir Henry Maine.[1]

> "The notion of what, for want of a better phrase, I must call a moral brotherhood in the whole human race, has been steadily gaining ground during the whole course of history, and we have now a large abstract term answering to this notion—Humanity."

It is clear at once that the word, as thus used, goes far beyond the Ciceronian usage, and it is not too much to say that it could not have been thus used, had not the mind of Comte enriched it before the middle of the nineteenth century. In this larger signification we have, first, three capital ideas which could hardly have been apprehended at all in classical times. There is the "brotherhood" of all,—the slave, the black man and the savage, as well as the cultivated gentlemen who practised the "humane" arts. There is the

[1] *Early History of Institutions*, p. 64.

189

idea of a progression of this ordered mankind throughout history, and the order rests on morality, i.e., it involves duties, with accompanying feelings which dictate appropriate actions. All this is implied in the modern usage which Comte did much to frame and to make explicit, and it by no means exhausts the fullness of his conception; in fact it does not include the capital point which would be called "metaphysical," had he not wished to ban that term from his philosophy. For, more than anyone, he gave vogue and substance to the idea that something comes into existence above and beyond every collectivity of men, about which we may rightly reason and make predictions, something more than we obtain by the mere numerical addition of all the items. The question has been fully argued by writers on social psychology and it is not necessary here to repeat the arguments.[1] It must suffice to say that what is generally recognized by the advocates of the nationality principle, and is true in various degrees of smaller units, such as the family or any other association of men, was predicated by Comte not only as possible and desirable, but as actually existent and growing in the case of Man as a

[1] See for instance, Paul Barth, *Die Philosophie der Geschichte als Soziologie.*

whole. On this conception the idea and worship of his Grand Etre were founded, and it is a grave, but unfortunately a frequent, error in studying Comte to be repelled by what seem to be the perversions of this use of worship and of Grand Etre, from recognizing the vital and much needed truth which underlies it.

The point is so characteristic and essential to Comte's whole scheme of thought that a little further illustration is desirable.

The best illustration is offered by the idea of the "Nation" as formulated and enforced by Comte's contemporary Hegel. This is both an illustration and an illuminating contrast. The "Nation" to Hegel and to many since, was "God walking on earth," that supreme thing to which all our actions should be subordinated, of which the will and the welfare afforded all the norm of conduct required. This divine authority was embodied in the constituted authorities of the day. It might be a legitimate government of long standing as in England; it might be a Hitler or a Mussolini who had made a sudden onslaught on the popular mind. The dictatorial cases are the extreme example, for there language is used and feelings cultivated which are only appropriate to the highest divine ideal which the mind can conceive. But some

fragment of the same order of thought and feeling
is present in every case of a man who dies for his
country, or claims that his country is the best
in the world, or acts, not because he wishes a
certain thing or thinks a certain thing right, but
because such and such is the standard or rule of
an Englishman. Now Comte's conception of
Humanity is only an extension and a purification
of this order of feelings and ideas. Theoretically,
it belongs to the same order of ideas; practically,
it is immeasurably harder to achieve, because the
area of the collectivity is so much greater, the
links connecting the items are so much weaker
and, above all, in Comte's case, there is involved
a spiritualization and a purification of the content.
He did not say, as the Hitlerite or the Fascist of
the moment, that the actual Nation embodied
in the living man was supreme or divine, but that
a Humanity, formed of all the best done and
thought in the history of man, was a power
above us to which we might rightly give allegiance, and in our turn do our best to elevate and
enrich. To some extent it is above us, whether
we will or no, just as the smaller being of the
Nation is above us in a closer sense. In Comte's
reading of history, the emergence and the growth
of this idea was the supreme fact, and, in his

religion, its cultivation and furtherance the highest duty.

We are not here dealing with the religious aspect of Comte's work but with the validity of his master-thought as it affects his view of history. But in each case the same question presses on the mind. Is there objective reality in this thing of which he speaks or is it a pure figment of the individual imagination? No doubt, it may be said, there have been countless myriads of human beings living, thinking and acting on the planet and we inherit what they have left us for good or ill. But a conception of the best, the constructive and vitalizing work which they have done, is as each mind may frame it. There is no ideal humanity except in the mind of the idealist individual. The answer can only follow the analogy with other forms of collective consciousness which was suggested above. In one sense it is perfectly true that any ideal or general conception is only consciously realized in individual minds. They alone have immediate knowledge of it. But it is untrue to infer from this that the collective thing has no other existence. The ideal conception of the nation persists and works in ways which we do not fully understand and it belongs to a special branch of sociology—that of social psychology—to investigate its workings. It has been remarked that the progress of peace and union in the world has been hampered by the want of suitable language, embodying the collective ideas of humanity and generally accepted. Nationalism has its burning vocabulary of "patriot" and "hero" and "motherland" to inspire the emotions. But no one can be stirred to the depths as an "internationalist," and the word "humanist" has so many different literary and educational connotations that its use in the more general sense is always difficult. The case is a good instance of the force of language in building up the collective intellectual life of men. Had there been a word conveying something of the passion and duty towards mankind as a whole, which "patriot" implies towards the motherland, there would have been fewer wars, less armaments and more unanimous vigour in the League of Nations.

It might have been hoped that, as Comte had the idea, he might have supplied the vocabulary, and in the word "humanity" he has indeed introduced a wealth of new and valuable associations. But "humanitarian" and "humanitarianism," coined on that basis, are vague as well as clumsy. Comte's own word to describe his system and his followers has attained wide currency with a different connotation. It introduces another leading idea which he has bequeathed to mankind and must now be considered as parallel to, and supporting, his conception of humanity.

His system was "positivism" and his method "positive."

Comte himself discovered seven different meanings for the word "positive,"[1] but the feat was rather a *tour de force*, and it is more helpful for understanding the real bearing of his thought to concentrate on the commonly accepted sense which it has borne to most of those who have reflected on his system since. It means, practically to everyone who uses it, either in French or English, "certain" or scientific, something which we can prove by reference to the evidence of our senses. A "positive" fact is one which everyone would admit, if he had an equal opportunity of judging. These are the "facts" on which science is built, as contrasted with things which we imagine or would like to see or believe. Now it is just the union of this order of thoughts with those represented by the word "humanity," which constitutes the unique quality of Comte's legacy to the world. Many before him and after

---

[1] *Appel aux Conservateurs*, p. 46.

have said, that men should love one another, that all were brothers or sons of one Father, that peace was the ideal destiny of mankind. Comte by linking the sentiment of humanity with the proved qualities of men and the historical development of his thought, put the ideal on a new basis of the real or positive. Man was in the process of becoming what the idealists had gradually foreseen. They had often foreseen it in part, but the steady evolution of positive thought gave substance and certainty to their vision. Hopes, if they can be fortified by science, become predictions.

A recent American writer[1] has stated the fundamental belief on which the "positivism" of Comte rested, in words so clear and emphatic that they deserve quotation and remembrance, at a time when we are informed in many quarters that the belief is obsolete. "We should regard nothing as outside the scope of science, and every regularity or law that science can discover in the consequence of events is a step towards the only freedom that is of use to men and an aid to the good life. If values do not reside in the orderly world of Nature, but depend on chance or caprice, it would be vain to try to increase them. The world needs, not only the vision and valuation

[1] Mr. E. L. Thorndike.

of great sages, and the practical psychology of men of affairs, but also scientific method to test the worth of the prophets' dreams, and scientific humanists to inform and advise its men of affairs, not only about what is, but also about what is right and good."

That is the gist of the second main thought which Comte has bequeathed to mankind. It was, of course, common to many other thinkers of his own time and since; but his special quality—in which no other man can be named beside him—lay in linking this belief with the growth of man in society. The belief had grown as man had grown; and Comte conceived it to be the primary function of sociology to make clear how this had taken place. If we can show, he thought, that the growth of scientific thought has sprung from the co-operation of all mankind and has tended to strengthen that co-operation;—this links up science with social progress. If we we can show, in the subject-matter of science, that regularities have been progressively discovered in all orders of facts till they come to include the facts of human society and history;—this gives us a stronger confidence in human thought, duly co-ordinated and tested. The two aspects support one another and are in fact the obverse and the reverse of the same medal. Humanity made by the progress of thought; thought exhibiting the reality and certain future of Humanity.

It is the word "certain," one of Comte's seven significations of "positive," which presents so much difficulty at the present day. There will be something to say about this in its more general aspect before we close. But two thoughts should be grasped firmly by those who wish to gain a wide and solid view of the whole matter as it presented itself to Comte. In the first place, the world has been passing through an extraordinary disturbance, due mainly to what we must, in the popular sense, call accidental causes. For who does not recognize that the Great War, from which we still suffer, hinged on the unregulated conflict of a few evil and extravagant wills? And who, surveying the recovery after the War is not amazed at the resilience and stability of the modern world? In the second place, for those who question "certainty," either in science or in society, a glance is recommended at the undisturbed mass of scientific construction which has gone on interruptedly, in spite either of mundane upheavals or of light talk about indeterminacy and the bankruptcy of thought. The progress of our knowledge of the material universe, based mainly on the synthesis of the seventeenth century, goes majestically forward. No actual worker at the subject would speak with less than awe of the contribution of Newton and his fellows, or doubts the regularity of the celestial phenomena. And in the other largest subdivision of scientific thought—the phenomena of life—though opinions are more divided and the facts are incomparably more complex, there is no faltering in the belief that laws or regularities may be discovered. In genetics indeed where most work has been done in recent times, the tendency has been even to an excess of mathematical regularity. There is no ground therefore for losing confidence in the second of Comte's leading thoughts.

A third master-thought is just as obvious as the first and second; it may even seem more universally pervasive in his mind than any other. It is the need for synthesis, great in his day, in some ways greater in our own. Like the positive spirit, it was by no means felt only by him; but he gave it a wider basis and a new application. The point requires some careful thinking and will be found to repay it, for it is a cardinal matter, both for the understanding of Comte's mind and in reference to many urgent questions in the intellectual state of the world to-day.

Practically, the social world has in many ways become more united or synthetic in its efforts in the last century. We have noted some of these symptoms in previous chapters,—the combined efforts of all civilized governments and communities to promote the welfare of their individual members, the union of the great majority of the nations in a common organization to secure common benefits, the mechanical knitting up of the globe and so forth. No one who realizes all this can be sceptical of the soundness of the humanitarian instinct or of Comte's advocacy of it on general lines. But when we turn to the intellectual basis on which all hope and effort rest, there is much more to be said and much less ground for satisfaction. And it is on this side that we should examine Comte's doctrine most carefully, because he had started the public exposition of his faith by asserting that right beliefs are prior to right actions. It was on this very ground that he had broken away from St.-Simon in his early manhood.

Intellectual synthesis is at the root of all science. Everyone who draws a fresh conclusion, whether he proceeds by induction or deduction, is bringing facts or ideas together, and by their union advancing to a new point of view. One need not refer to any special system of logic for confirmation of this truth; it is patent in all of them. The mind is always seeking and finding fresh unity in fresh diversities. Hence the progress of science is itself a demonstration of the fundamental need and constant triumph of synthesis. But when we examine more closely the various types of fact, between which unities are established, we are brought face to face with two profound differences on both of which Comte laid great stress, and of which the latter has a grave moral lesson for mankind. As we ascend in the order of phenomena, from the simplest, such as the number and size of things, to the most complex, such as the facts of life or the thoughts of men, we find increasing change and incomparably greater diversity. Hence men have, from the first, been able to bring their synthetic powers to play and to establish regularities, more quickly and safely in the former class than in the latter, and in all the intermediate facts according to their complexity. This is, as we saw, the broad basis for Comte's classification of the sciences. But, side by side with the growing complexity, as we ascend the scale, another difference or principle is to be noted which ultimately comes in aid of the great goal of synthesis, as men become aware, and make use, of it. The more complex are also the more modifiable by human, or other living, effort. We cannot alter the courses of the stars but we may make gardens in a wilderness, breed new varieties of horses or of apples, and by a supreme effort control our own passions. In all such cases we should not speak of indeterminacy: the human will comes in as one of the determining causes.

Now Comte's synthesis was avowedly and strongly based on the control of the more complex order of events by the application of a conscious human will. He would have had an economy of human effort by saving thought on matters which could have no bearing on human welfare, in order to devote more to the directly human good. His conception of what might have this bearing was too narrow, and its failure in the one conspicuous case of astrophysics has often been used to discredit his name. It is far more useful to lay stress on the vital and necessary truths which have been obscured by such mistakes in detail. No doubt valuable truths have often been arrived at on paths which seem to diverge from human ends. But it is equally true, and a hideous fact, that vast efforts are being expended daily on objects which have not only no direct bearing on human welfare, but aim consciously at destroying it. The by-products reached by the manufacture of poison gas or the perfecting of bombing-engines cannot redeem the waste and wickedness of such research, and it is good to see that in this matter the consciences of many men of science are now awake. Without any narrow conception of the utility of research, it is possible to check the positively harmful and encourage the beneficial. Moreover, if man is the highest known manifestation of the ideal on earth, the furtherance of that ideal in him, must, broadly conceived, be the canon of all action and all thought.

It is on the level of thought that it is most difficult to attain the synthesis which Comte, in common with many others, was always striving to promote. We have indicated his own recipe—the good of man—on previous pages in many places. But as the question is the largest and most difficult which arises from his teaching, and also that on which least apparent progress has been made since his day, it may be well to add a few explanatory words. The dispersion and specialization of research, already marked in his time, is vastly greater now. Sociology, which was to have been the supreme unifier of science, has become itself a science with many subdivisions. Whatever our ultimate ideal of the good, no one can think it furthered by the seclusion of all the little bands of thinkers, each in his own cabin. Comte had his own specific for the evil. There should be another class of specialists, specializing in generalities, and a few eminently useful men stand out in England and elsewhere, attempting valiantly to grapple with this task. But England, so apt to co-operate on the practical plane, is specially recalcitrant on the plane of general ideas. They should, the typical Englishman would say, be left to look after themselves, while actual human beings should aim at knowing and doing one thing well. A change no doubt will come, but it will come slowly. As the sphere in which the change is needed is the most complex as well as the most abstract, it is, on Comte's showing, that in which the concentration of the mind and will are most called for and would be most effective. Those who have a glimmering of the truth, must think hard and endeavour to gain others to think with them. There is no other way.

The deepest cleavage remains where it was, and it is unfortunately in that realm of thought on which most depends, the field in which Comte discovered the guiding line of common thought, developing and uniting mankind. If history is still to be regarded as the account of the rise and government of states, the hope of a common consciousness in mankind must be long delayed. History, primarily regarded as the history of the development of the human mind, is the sole main road to intellectual synthesis. The side-roads may diverge and come back again, but unless the main direction is secured, there can be no certainty of the goal.

That Comte has stood practically alone, assuredly the most eminent, in pointing this way to attain the concentration and harmony of individual and national minds which all admit to be profoundly needed at the present day, is one of his most signal services. Educationally, it is the greatest. The other master both of science and of sociology, most famous in Comte's day, Herbert Spencer, entirely missed this point. He had the science in large measure, but he had no history. History as he saw it, was a mass of unmeaning and unessential details. He could not imagine that, illumined by a true theory, much of it might take light. Comte, with all the limitations and errors that we may find in him, saw and made light, and we should do well to go back and light a candle at his flame.

It is interesting to note that, just fifty years ago, a distinguished Hegelian philosopher, Edward

Caird, Master of Balliol, went back to Comte in much this spirit, and has recorded his impressions in a book,[1] which, in spite of all its criticism, is perhaps the most sympathetic and understanding account of Comte to be found in English. What he says, in appreciation, accords so well with what has been said above, and throughout this book, that a few of his sentences may fitly serve as a summary and epilogue.

"It was Comte's own best achievement to apply this idea (of the unity of the universal and particular) to one great department of science (i.e., sociology). It was to show that society, whether in the form of the family, of the nation, or of humanity, is not merely a collection of similar individuals, but a unity of organically related members; and that its development is not merely a succession of events, but the evolution of one life which remains identical with itself through all its changes.

"By knowing other things and beings as directly as we know ourselves, our subjectivity is no longer a limit to us, and a 'subjective' synthesis may be at the same time 'objective.' . . . We are 'a part of all that we have known' and all that we have known is a part of us. Our

[1] *The Social Philosophy and Religion of Comte.* E. Caird, 1885.

life widens with our world and is indeed the
same thing from an opposite point of view. . . .
We are forced to recognize that the consciousness of self lifts us to a universal or central
point of view—a point of view which is central,
not merely in relation to one's own feeling and
states, but central also in relation to the objective
world. The being who knows himself as an
individual, is for that very reason not merely
individual; he can know a reality which is
not merely that of his own subjective states or
sensations and can identify himself with an end
which is not merely his own expected pleasure.
. . . As he is the most complex and dependent
of existences, we can only rise to a satisfactory
knowledge of him after we have laid a basis
for this knowledge in the study of the simpler
phenomena of the organic and inorganic world.
But, on the other hand, the possibility of all
this objective science—of the knowledge by
man of that which is not man—lies in this,
that he is not merely part of the whole—not
merely the most complex existence in the world
—but that the universal principle, the principle
which gives unity to the world, manifests itself in him. It is because, as has been said,
'Nature becomes conscious of itself in man'

that man in his turn can read the open secret
of Nature. In spelling out the meaning of
nature and history, he is taking the only true
way, and indeed the only way, to the knowledge of himself; but this knowledge would be
to him impossible, if the self-consciousness that
makes him man, were not also the principle
of unity in the objective world. Comte himself
has an obscure perception of this truth when
he says that 'strictly speaking there is no
phenomenon within our experience which is not
in the truest sense human . . . for man sums
up in himself all the laws of the world as the
ancients truly felt.' . . . It follows from this
that the last science, the science of man, in so
far as it is also the science of mind, cannot
merely be built upon and added to the physical
and natural sciences, but must react upon them
and transform them. For, though the knowledge
of man presupposes the knowledge of nature,
yet on the other hand the knowledge of nature
which we get when we abstract from it its
relation to man, is imperfect and incomplete.
The true idea of nature cannot be attained
except when it is viewed in relation to that being
who is at once its culmination and its explanation. . . . Hence all the sciences which treat of

the mathematical, physical and vital relations of things, must be regarded as hypothetical, and based upon abstraction, for thought, spirit, mind is implied in all such relations nor can a complete or adequate conception of them be attained until we have regarded the self-consciousness that makes us men, as, in this point of view, not only the last but also the first, not merely the end, but also the beginning of nature. In this sense the analytic separation of the sciences from each other, and from thought, must be modified and corrected in a final synthesis which will indeed be 'subjective,' in so far as it brings into view the unity of the subject pre-supposed in all knowledge. But to one who has understood the full meaning of the process, this 'subjective synthesis' will be also objective. . . . Now it is Comte's merit that he altogether repudiates that false subjective synthesis which was the natural result of the principles of Locke and Berkeley. Rejecting the doctrine that what we know immediately is only the states of our own consciousness, he takes his stand at an objective point of view and arranges the sciences in an objective order, which begins with the inorganic world and ends with man as the most complex of all existences. On the other hand, it is his merit that he sees the necessity of that true 'subjective synthesis' which arises from the reaction of the last science, the science of man upon those that went before it, or, in other words from the perception that man is not merely the end, but also in a sense, the beginning of nature.

"The external fatality (of nature) can no longer be called unfriendly, or even indifferent, to man; or rather its immediate appearance as his enemy is the condition of its being in a higher sense his friend. Kant, in his short treatise on history (with which Comte was acquainted and which probably had no little influence upon the *Politique Positive*) applies a similar thought to the struggles and competition of mankind with each other. The very selfish rivalry of men, he contended, is in the long run the means of developing a higher sociality than could have existed among a race of beings with whom personal feeling was at first less intense. . . . No conclusion unfavourable to Optimism in any high sense of the word can be founded on the fact that the world is not arranged for the immediate happiness of man, if that immediate happiness would have been purchased by his moral degradation; or even if it would have been less powerful to call forth the higher energies of his nature. . . . The best kind of Optimism has not been based upon a shallow and imperfect view of the misery, still less of the moral evil, of man's life. Rather it has been attained through the clearest perception of both. It has been an Optimism that has descended into the grave of human happiness, into the 'hell' of human guilt, that it might rise again 'leading captivity Captive.'"

The vision is true and moving; the appreciation of Comte touches his most permanent and vital side. "Nature comes to self-consciousness in Man!" So far the Comtian synthesis may be fairly expressed in terms acceptable to Caird or Hegel. When they go further, and say "Therefore the process of man's life is a continuation of the self-revelation of the Absolute Being which begins in Nature," Comte merely asks whether the statement adds anything to our comprehension of the universe, in which our mind has been born and lives and thrives. It thrives, he would say, not on formulæ without positive meaning, but on the fruit of an earnest quest, seizing the new fact and testing it, using the result for the structure of a living thing, with infinite capacities for the future. For the rest, the leading ideas which have appeared in this chapter, may be found in some measure in many other thinkers since philosophy began, with growing frequency as we approach our own day. But they are found united in the fullest measure in the thought of Comte. Humanity is there, as the necessary ideal in any comprehensive scheme of thought, whether we use that term or not. Science appears as the directing force, already enlarged, and to be enlarged, far beyond the dreams of Comte who gave it that prerogative place. Synthesis, or the unity both of thought and feeling, assumes with him a more solid meaning, because while the basis must be love, the structure is bound together by intellectual ties and the progress of science is at every step a further proof of the triumph of synthesis. Hope, or Faith in the Future, also takes on with him a more substantial shape than with the pure idealist, for, fortified by science, it may begin to predict, which is the mark of science.

Humanity, Science, Synthesis, Faith in the Future; this is the final chord, with Humanity as the dominant note.

DATES IN COMTE'S LIFE

Birth at Montpellier, 1798
Lamarck's "Philosophie Zoologique," 1809
Comte enters Polytechnic School, 1814
Relations with St. Simon, 1818–24
Earliest works, 1819–28
"Système de Philosophie Positive," 1830–42
Occupies posts at Polytechnic School, 1832–44
Friendship with Mme de Vaux, 1845–46
Revolution in France and Comte's institution of a Free Association for the Positive Education of the West, 1848
Death, 1857

A FEW BOOKS FOR REFERENCE

In French, the best fairly recent, sympathetic appreciation of Comte's philosophy is Lévy-Bruhl's *La Philosophie de Auguste Comte* (Alcan). Littré's *Auguste Comte et la Philosophie Positive*, remains indispensable for the facts of his career, and, while independent in its personal judgment, is sympathetic philosophically.

In English, Harriet Martineau's *Positive Philosophy of Auguste Comte: freely translated and condensed*, gives a quite adequate general account. The whole work in six volumes has not been translated, but the *Positive Polity* in four volumes was very carefully rendered by Messrs. Bridges, Harrison, Bessly and Congreve. John Stuart Mill's *Auguste Comte and Positivism* is the later criticism of an old and ardent admirer, interesting, penetrating and outspoken.

Edward Caird's *Social Philosophy and Religion of Comte* is a sympathetic estimate from the neo-Hegelian point of view.

The best, entirely friendly and illuminating, comments are to be found in Dr. J. H. Bridges' *Illustrations of Positivism* (Watts), while a careful and interesting account of the English religious movement inspired by Comte is given in an American thesis called *A Crusade for Humanity* by John Edwin McGee.

INDEX